Java Transaction
Design Strategies

Written by
Mark Richards

C4Media, Publisher of InfoQ.com.
Part of the InfoQ Enterprise Software Development series.

For information or ordering of this or other InfoQ books, please contact
books@c4media.com.

Production Credits:
Managing Editor: Floyd Marinescu
Cover art: Gene Steffanson
Composition: Melissa Tessier & Chris Olsen

Library of Congress Cataloging-in-Publication Data:

ISBN: 978-1-4116-9591-7

Printed in the United States of America

10 9 8 7 6 5 3 2 1

Acknowledgements

I would like to thank Alan Beaulieu (author of *Learning SQL* and co-author of *Mastering Oracle SQL*) and Stuart Dabbs Halloway (author of *Component Development for the Java Platform*) for reviewing the book from the very first chapter and for supporting me throughout this project. Your technical and editorial feedback has been both helpful and insightful (and sometimes humorous as well!). I would also like to thank Mark Little (author of *Java Transaction Processing*) for reviewing the final draft manuscript and for providing me with excellent technical comments and suggestions. Your detailed review and willingness to take the time to discuss various technical aspects of the book was very helpful and definitely added to the finishing touches of the book. I would also like to particularly acknowledge and thank Floyd Marinescu (creator of TheServerSide.com and author of *EJB Design Patterns*) for publishing this book and for providing excellent guidance and feedback throughout this project. Your technical and editorial suggestions were right on target and made this a much better book than it would have been without your help.

Most of all, I would like to thank my wonderful wife Rebecca for supporting me throughout this project. From your help with reviewing the first chapters of the initial manuscript to your never-ending support throughout the project, you provided me with the encouragement and confidence I needed to complete this book. Now that it is finished I promise I will try to spend more time away from the computer when I am at home (right - like *that* is ever going to happen!).

Contents

1

Introduction

There are many varieties of custom enterprise Java applications that exist in the world today. While some of these applications are simple web-based applications leveraging a few local Java-Beans or POJOs (Plain Old Java Objects), many are sophisticated n-tiered applications using commercial or open source application servers leveraging frameworks such as remote Enterprise Java Beans (EJBs), messaging using JMS (Java Messaging Service), or even Spring. While some of these sophisticated enterprise applications work fine, most seem to suffer from random and sometimes unexplainable data integrity problems including incorrect account balances, multiple orders shipped to a customer, orders "lost" by the system, and general data synchronization issues between tables in a database. These types of problems are usually caused by an ineffective or missing transaction management strategy.

As a seasoned veteran, I find that most enterprise Java applications I come across do not have an effective transaction design strategy or simply rely on the database to manage complex transactions. I frequently ask architects and developers to describe their overall transaction management design strategy. Whether using EJB or the Spring Framework, the response I usually get is that they use *Declarative Transactions*. As we will learn from this book, the term *Declarative Transactions* refers to a transaction model that can be used as the basis for managing transactions, but is certainly not a transaction design strategy by itself.

Developers, designers, and architects should be concerned about transaction processing mainly because there are three things we can be guaranteed of in life; death, taxes, and system failures. Aside from being cryogenically frozen like Austin Powers there isn't much we can do about death, and taxes are unavoidable regardless how long we live. Fortunately, there is something we can do about system failures. Understanding how transaction management works in Java and developing an effective transaction design strategy can help to avoid data integrity problems in your applications and databases and ease the pain of inevitable system failures.

As the title suggests, this book is about *how* to design an effective transaction management strategy using the transaction models provided by Java-based frameworks such as EJB and Spring. Although I will be going into details about each transaction model, those particular chapters are really meant to describe the techniques, best practices, and pitfalls within each model. The transaction design pattern chapters of the book bring all these concepts and techniques together and describe *how* to use these models to effectively manage transactions within your EJB or Spring-based Java applications.

As the famous mathematician Blaise Pascal once wrote, "I have made this letter longer than usual, because I lack the time to make it short". Most readers do not have the time or the patience to read a verbose book about transaction management. To that end, the purpose of this book is to present, *in a concise manner*, the information an architect and developer needs to know to build an effective transaction design strategy for both small and large-scale enterprise Java applications, regardless of the framework you are using. My goal in writing this book is to help the reader understand each of the transaction models, understand the best practices within those models, learn about transaction design patterns, and understand how to apply transaction design patterns to various application architectures.
I will be illustrating the transaction management concepts described in this book using examples from EJB 2.1, EJB 3.0, and

the Spring Framework. While a complete account of all the details of transaction processing in either of these frameworks and corresponding persistence frameworks is beyond the scope of this book, it is my hope that the concepts and examples shown in this book will provide the reader with enough details to understand the concepts and implementation techniques to build a more effective transaction design strategy.

Transaction Models

Whether you are using Spring or EJB, it is important to understand the various transaction models that are available. The three transaction models available for transaction management in Java are the Local Transaction Model, Programmatic Transaction Model, and the Declarative Transaction Model. Although I will be devoting a chapter for each of these models, I thought it might be useful to first provide a brief summary of each.

The *Local Transaction Model* gets its name from the fact that it is not really the framework that is managing the transaction, but rather the local resource manager. The resource manager is the actual provider of the data source with which you are communicating. For example, for databases the resource manager is implemented through the database driver and DBMS. For JMS, the resource manager is the queue (or topic) connection factory implemented through the particular JMS provider. With the Local Transaction Model the developer manages *connections*, not *transactions*. It is the DBMS or JMS Provider that is actually managing the local transaction. I will be discussing the details of the Local Transaction Model in chapter two.

The *Programmatic Transaction Model* leverages the power of the Java Transaction API (JTA) and the underlying transaction service implementation to provide transactional support without the limitations of the Local Transaction Model. With the Programmatic Transaction Model the developer writes code that manages *transactions* rather than *connections*. Using the `javax.transaction.UserTransaction` interface, the developer codes the `begin()` method to start the transaction and either the `commit()` or `rollback()` method to terminate the transaction. Although the use of programmatic transactions is discouraged, it is still sometimes used within EJB for client-initiated transactions that access remote Stateless SessionBeans. We will be taking a much closer look at this transaction model in chapter three of the book.

The *Declarative Transaction Model*, otherwise known as Container-Managed Transactions (or CMT) in the EJB world, is the primary transaction model I will be focusing on throughout this book. With the Declarative Model the framework or container manages the starting and stopping (i.e. commit or rollback) of the transaction. Developers only need to tell the framework when to rollback the transaction on application exceptions and configure the transaction through configuration parameters found in XML deployment descriptors (e.g. `ejb-jar.xml`) in EJB or the bean definition file (e.g. `ApplicationContext.xml`) in Spring. The details of the Declarative Transaction Model are covered in chapter four of the book.

Where's the ACID, Man?

If we were in the 1960s this would probably be the most popular section in the book. However, in today's technology world ACID means something different than in did in the 1960s. ACID is an acronym used to describe the desired properties of a transaction. These properties are **A**tomicity, **C**onsistency, **I**solation, and **D**urability.

The *Atomicity* property means a transaction must either commit or rollback *all* of its updates in a single unit of work. Regardless of the number of updates made, all updates must be treated as a collective whole. This property is sometimes referred to as a LUW (Logical Unit of Work) or SUW (Single Unit of Work).

The *Consistency* property means that during the course of an active transaction the database will never be left in an inconsistent state. This means every time an insert, update, or delete is performed on the database during a transaction the integrity constraints in the database are applied, even though the transaction has not yet been committed. This can have consequences to developers. For example, the consistency property implies that during a transaction you cannot add a detail record without first adding a summary record. Although some databases allow you defer constraint checking until commit time, generally you cannot violate a foreign key constraint during the course of a transaction, even if you intend on correcting the condition during the latter part of the transaction.

The *Isolation* property refers to the degree to which individual transactions interact with each other. This ACID property determines how protected *my* uncommitted updates from *other* transactions accessing the same information. Isolation is a function of consistency and concurrency. As the level of isolation increases, consistency increases and concurrency decreases. I will be going into more detail about transaction isolation in chapter 4.

The *Durability* property of transactions means that when we receive a successful commit from a transaction we are guaranteed that the transaction is complete and the database or JMS updates are permanent and will survive a system failure (like spilling a bottle of beer on the server console or bringing the server farm down due to playing our favorite multi-player game). Some of the modern sophisticated caching strategies used by several major database vendors could question the durability of some updates, but in general when we receive a successful commit message we can be guaranteed that our updates are permanent and cannot be lost.

JTA and JTS

To effectively manage transactions in enterprise Java applications developers do not necessarily need to know the behind-the-scenes details of the Java Transaction Service (JTS) specification. However, regardless whether you are using EJB or Spring, it is important to understand the limitations that exist with respect to distributed transaction processing in Java.

Regardless of the framework you are using, most enterprise Java applications leverage the Java Transaction API (JTA) for transaction management. The JTA is the interface developers use to manage transactions. The Java Transaction Service (JTS), on the other hand, is an underlying transaction service that implements JTA and is used by most commercial and opens source application servers (note that there are other transaction services on the market besides JTS that can be used). Think of the relationship between JTA and JTS as similar to the relationship between JDBC and the corresponding underlying database driver; JTA is to JDBC as JTS is to the database driver. The JTA can be implemented through commercial application servers or through open source transaction managers such as the JBoss Transaction Service (http://www.jboss.com/products/transactions) or JOTM (http://jotm.objectweb.org/).

The Java Transaction Service (JTS) is the Java language mapping of the CORBA OTS 1.1 Specification (Object Transaction Service). As a developer this is not terribly important, unless you are playing some bizarre version of Trivial Pursuit or in a real tough job interview. Although JTS is not mandated by J2EE, it is mandatory for the interoperability of distributed transactions between heterogeneous implementations. Because the JTA must support both JTS and non-JTS implementations, it is often difficult to tell the precise functionality supported by an implementation simply by looking at the JTA interfaces. For example, although the JTS specification has optional support for nested transactions, J2EE does not support this feature. You cannot distinguish these differences from looking at the JTA.

Fortunately, there are not many interfaces a developer needs to be concerned about when dealing with transactions. For example, when using Programmatic Transactions, the only interface we need to use is the `javax.transaction.UserTransaction` interface. This interface allows us to programmatically begin a transaction, commit a transaction, rollback a transaction, and get the transaction status. When using Declarative Transactions in EJB we are primarily concerned with the `setRollbackOnly()` method in the `EJBContext` Interface. There is much more we can do with the interfaces provided by the `javax.transaction` package, but developers wouldn't use these very often. For example, as we will see further in this book there are times when may need direct access to the transaction manager. These situations occur when we need to manually suspend or resume a transaction when using Declarative Transactions. We can also start, commit, and rollback the transaction using the `TransactionManager` interface.

UserTransaction Interface

The `UserTransaction` interface is only used in the Programmatic Transaction Model, primarily within EJB. The only methods in this interface the developer needs to be concerned about are the following:

- `begin()`
- `commit()`
- `rollback()`
- `getStatus()`

javax.transaction.UserTransaction.begin()
The `begin()` method is used in the Programmatic Transaction Model to start a new transaction and associate the transaction with the current thread. This method will throw a `NotSupportedException` if it is called when a transaction is already

associated with the current thread and the underlying transaction service does not support nested transactions.

javax.transaction.UserTransaction.commit()
The commit() method is used in the Programmatic Transaction Model to commit the transaction associated with the current thread and terminate the transaction. This method will also disassociate the transaction with the current thread. In Java only a single transaction may be associated with the current thread. Under XA this method may throw a HeuristicMixedException or HeuristicRollbackException, indicating that the resource manager made a decision independent of the transaction manager to either rollback or make partial commits to the transaction between phases one and two of the two-phase commit process. I will be discussing two-phase commit and heuristic exception processing in more detail in Chapter 5 of this book.

javax.transaction.UserTransaction.rollback()
The rollback() method is used in the Programmatic Transaction Model to rollback the transaction associated with the current thread and terminate the transaction. The rollback() method will also disassociate the transaction from the current thread.

javax.transaction.UserTransaction.getStatus()
The getStatus() method is used in the Programmatic Transaction Model to return an integer value indicating the status of the current transaction. The integer return value is quite meaningless at first glance, but we can use the javax.transaction.Status interface to determine what status is being returned from the getStatus() method. I will be discussing the javax.transaction.Status interface in detail later in this chapter.

TransactionManager Interface

The javax.transaction.TransactionManager interface is primarily used within the Declarative Transaction Model. For programmatic transactions you can do essentially everything with the `TransactionManager` interface as you can with the `UserTransaction` interface. However, with most methods it is better to use the `UserTransaction` interface and leave the `TransactionManager` interface alone unless you need to suspend or resume a transaction.

javax.transaction.TransactionManager.suspend()
The `suspend()` method is used in the Declarative or Programmatic Transaction Model to suspend the transaction associated with the current thread. This method returns a reference to the current transaction or null if no transaction is associated with the current thread. This method is useful if we need to suspend the current transaction to execute some code or a stored procedure that is not compatible with XA. We will see an example of the use of this method in Chapter 5 of the book.

javax.transaction.TransactionManager.resume()
The `resume()` method is used in the Declarative or Programmatic Transaction Model to resume a previously suspended transaction. It takes as an argument a reference to the previously suspended transaction, associates that transaction with the current thread, and then resumes the transaction.

EJBContext Interface

The `EJBContext()` interface is used in the Declarative Transaction Model within EJB and contains only one method that is useful in transaction management, which is the `setRollbackOnly()` method.

javax.ejb.EJBContext.setRollbackOnly()
The `setRollbackOnly()` method is used in the Declarative Transaction Model to notify the container that the only possible outcome for the current transaction is for it to rollback. The interesting thing about this method is that it does not actually rollback the transaction upon invocation; it only *marks* the trans-

action for rollback, which produces the STATUS_MARKED_ROLLBACK status from the getStatus() method. The same results can be achieved through the TransactionManager.setRollbackOnly() method, but since we already have the SessionContext or MessageDrivenContext it makes sense to use this method instead.

Status Interface

As we saw in the previous section, we can obtain the status of the transaction through the javax.transaction.Status interface as a result of the value obtained from the UserTransaction.getStatus() method. I am devoting a section to the transaction status because first it is sort of cool and second because it provides us with a lot of useful information regarding the state of the current transaction. The following values are contained in the status interface:

- STATUS_ACTIVE
- STATUS_COMMITTED
- STATUS_COMMITTING
- STATUS_MARKED_ROLLBACK
- STATUS_NO_TRANSACTION
- STATUS_PREPARED
- STATUS_PREPARING
- STATUS_ROLLEDBACK
- STATUS_ROLLING_BACK
- STATUS_UNKNOWN

Out of all the status values listed above, the only ones that are really useful to developers in most mainstream Java business applications are STATUS_ACTIVE, STATUS_MARKED_ROLLBACK and STATUS_NO_TRANSACTION. The following sections describe these status values in more detail and how they might be useful.

STATUS_ACTIVE

There may be times when it is important to see if a current transaction is associated with the thread. For example, for debugging and optimization purposes we may want to add an aspect or interceptor to check for the presence of a transaction during query operations. Using this aspect and status value we can detect possible optimizations to our transaction design strategy. Other times we may want to use this status if we need to suspend the current transaction or execute code that would cause our application to fail (such as executing a stored procedure containing DDL code under XA). The following code snippet shows the use of the STATUS_ACTIVE status value:

```
...
if (txn.getStatus() == Status.STATUS_ACTIVE)
   logger.info("Transaction active in query operation");
...
```

In this example we have logic that will create an entry in the log file if we have a transaction in the query method. This might be an indication that we have a transaction when we do not need one, thereby identifying a possible optimization opportunity or problem with our overall transaction design strategy.

STATUS_MARKED_ROLLBACK

This status may be useful when working with the Declarative Transaction Model. For performance optimization reasons we may want to skip processing if the transaction has been marked for rollback in a previous method call. Therefore, if we want to see whether the transaction has been marked for rollback, we can check it as shown in the code example below:

```
...
if (txn.getStatus() == Status.STATUS_MARKED_ROLLBACK)
  throw new Exception(
    "Further Processing Halted Due To Txn Rollback");
...
```

STATUS_NO_TRANSACTION

This status is useful because it is the only way to determine if there truly is no transaction context. Like the STATUS_ACTIVE, this can also be used for debugging or optimization purposes to check for the presence of a transaction where there should be one. Using as aspect or interceptor (or inline code) we could detect possible holes in our transaction design strategy for those methods that require an update. The following code example shows the use of the STATUS_NO_TRANSACTION value:

```
...
if (txn.getStatus() == Status.STATUS_NO_TRANSACTION)
    throw new Exception(
        "Transaction needed but none exists");
...
```

Notice that we cannot simply check to see if the status is not equal to the STATUS_ACTIVE state because the lack of this status does not indicate the lack of a transaction context. There could be a transaction context in one of the other states listed above.

Summary

The next three chapters focus on the different transaction models. Although the concepts in this book are primarily illustrated through EJB, I have provided examples in Spring as well. While complete examples in all of the persistence frameworks is well beyond the scope of this book, I would encourage you to read this book to understand the concepts, tips, pitfalls, and best practices of these transaction models, and then turn to the documentation for your specific persistence framework for further implementation details.

2

The Local Transaction Model

The term *Local Transactions* refers to the fact that transaction management is handled by the underlying Database (DBMS) or in the case of JMS the underlying messaging provider. From a developer perspective we do not manage *transactions* within the Local Transaction Model, but rather *connections*. The code example below illustrates the use of the Local Transaction Model using straight JDBC code:

```
public void updateTradeOrder(TradeOrderData order)
    throws Exception {
    DataSource ds = (DataSource)
        (new InitialContext()).lookup("jdbc/MasterDS");
    Connection conn = ds.getConnection();
    conn.setAutoCommit(false);
    Statement stmt = conn.createStatement();
    String sql = "update trade_order ... ";
    try {
        stmt.executeUpdate(sql);
        conn.commit();
    } catch (Exception e) {
        conn.rollback();
        throw e;
    } finally {
        stmt.close();
        conn.close();
    }
}
```

Notice in the above example the use of the `Connection.setAutoCommit(false)` in conjunction with the `Connection.commit()` and `Connection.rollback()` methods. The `setAutoCommit()` method is a very important part of the overall developer-based connection management. The auto commit flag tells the underlying DBMS whether or not it should commit the connection immediately after the execution of each SQL statement. A value of true tells the DBMS to commit or rollback the connection immediately after the execution of each SQL statement, whereas a value of false will keep the connection active and not commit the changes until an explicit `commit()` is executed. By default this flag is usually set to *true*. Therefore, by default if we have multiple SQL updates, each of them will be executed and committed independently from each other and the `Connection.commit()` and `Connection.rollback()` statements will be ignored.

For low-level JDBC coding in the Spring Framework you would simply use the `org.springframework.jdbc.datasource.DataSourceUtils` as shown in the coding example below:

```
public void updateTradeOrder(TradeOrderData order)
    throws Exception {
    Connection conn = DataSourceUtils
                     .getConnection(dataSource);
    conn.setAutoCommit(false);
    Statement stmt = conn.createStatement();
    String sql = "update trade_order ... ";
    try {
        stmt.executeUpdate(sql);
        conn.commit();
    } catch (Exception e) {
        conn.rollback();
        throw e;
    } finally {
        stmt.close();
        conn.close();
    }
}
```

In Spring, the datasource and corresponding business object would be defined in the Spring configuration file as follows:

```
<bean id="datasource"
  class="org.springframework.jndi.JndiObjectFactoryBean">
    <property name="jndiName" value="jdbc/MasterDS"/>
```

```
</bean>

<bean id="TradingService"
      class="com.trading.server.TradingService">
    <property name="dataSource">
      <ref local="datasource"/>
    </property>
</bean>
```

For the remaining code examples in this chapter, if you are using Spring you can replace the DataSource lookup and getConnection() method with the code listed above.

Auto Commit and Connection Management

The auto commit flag is a very important element within the Local Transaction Model, *regardless of whether you are using EJB or Spring*. By default this flag is usually set to true, indicating that the DBMS should commit (or rollback) the connection after each update SQL statement. Consider the JDBC code example below. This code has a single SQL update with no programmatic connection management. Because the auto commit flag is set to true (by default), the underlying DBMS will manage the connection and commit or rollback the updates.

```
public void updateTradeOrder(TradeOrderData order)
    throws Exception {
    DataSource ds = (DataSource)
      (new InitialContext()).lookup("jdbc/MasterDS");
    Connection conn = ds.getConnection();
    Statement stmt = conn.createStatement();
    String sql = "update trade_order ... ";
    try {
      stmt.executeUpdate(sql);
    } catch (Exception e) {
      throw e;
    } finally {
      stmt.close();
      conn.close();
    }
}
```

The code above works because there is only a single SQL update in the method. However, let's assume we have multiple update statements to execute in the *same method* as illustrated below.

```
public void updateTradeOrder(TradeOrderData order)
    throws Exception {
    double fee = calculateFee(order);
    DataSource ds = (DataSource)
        (new InitialContext()).lookup("jdbc/MasterDS");
    Connection conn = ds.getConnection();
    Statement stmt = conn.createStatement();
    String sqlOrder = "update trade_order ... ";
    String sqlTrade = "update trade_fee ... ";
    try {
        stmt.executeUpdate(sqlOrder);
        stmt.executeUpdate(sqlTrade);
    } catch (Exception e) {
        throw e;
    } finally {
        stmt.close();
        conn.close();
    }
}
```

In the example above we added additional code to recalculate the fee associated with the trade and to update the corresponding table to record the new fee associated with this trade order. As it is written this code compiles and executes, but does not support ACID properties. First, because by default the auto commit flag is true, the connection will be committed after the execution of the first executeUpdate() method. If the second executeUpdate() statement failed, the method would throw an exception but the first SQL update would be committed, thus violating the atomicity property of ACID. Second, these updates, as part of a logical unit of work (LUW) are not isolated from other processing that might be accessing the same tables or rows, thus violating the isolation property of ACID.

To make the above code work properly from a transaction and LUW perspective, we must set the auto commit flag to false and add connection commit and rollback logic to the code. By setting the auto commit flag to false we are telling the underlying DBMS that we will manage the connections and code the commit() and rollback() methods ourselves. In this manner we can group SQL updates together in a single logical unit of work within a single atomic transaction. The listing below shows an example of how to manage multiple updates:

```
public void updateTradeOrder(TradeOrderData order)
    throws Exception {
    double fee = calculateFee(order);
    DataSource ds = (DataSource)
        (new InitialContext()).lookup("jdbc/MasterDS");
    Connection conn = ds.getConnection();
    conn.setAutoCommit(false);
    Statement stmt = conn.createStatement();
    String sqlOrder = "update trade_order ... ";
    String sqlTrade = "update trade_fee ... ";
    try {
        stmt.executeUpdate(sqlOrder);
        stmt.executeUpdate(sqlTrade);
        conn.commit();
    } catch (Exception e) {
        conn.rollback();
        throw e;
    } finally {
        stmt.close();
        conn.close();
    }
}
```

By adding the `conn.setAutoCommit(false)` and the `commit()` and `rollback()` methods in the code above the two SQL updates will be treated as a single unit of work.

To illustrate the deficiencies with the Local Transaction Model, consider the code example below where we move the SQL updates into separate DAO (Data Access Object) methods:

```
public void updateTradeOrder(TradeOrderData order)
    throws Exception {
    OrderDAO orderDao = new OrderDAO();
    TradeDAO tradeDao = new TradeDAO();
    try {
        //SQL and Connection Logic in DAO Classes
        orderDao.update(order);
        tradeDao.update(order);
    } catch (Exception e) {
        logger.fatal(e);
        throw e;
    }
}
```

The `OrderDAO` and `TradeDAO` objects contain the SQL and connection logic found in the earlier code examples. In this example, regardless of the auto commit settings or connection management in each DAO method, each update is handled separately. This means that the database updates will be committed after each DAO update() method.

One might be tempted to solve this problem using a technique known as *connection passing*. With connection passing we establish a database connection at the higher-level method, and pass the connection into the DAO update() methods. Using connection passing we could modify the code example above to pass connections, making our code ACID compliant. The following code shows an example of using connection passing.

```
public void updateTradeOrder(TradeOrderData order)
    throws Exception {
    DataSource ds = (DataSource)
        (new InitialContext()).lookup("jdbc/MasterDS");
    Connection conn = ds.getConnection();
    conn.setAutoCommit(false);
    OrderDAO orderDao = new OrderDAO();
    TradeDAO tradeDao = new TradeDAO();
    try {
        //SQL and Connection Logic in DAO Classes
        orderDao.update(order, conn);
        tradeDao.update(order, conn);
        conn.commit();
    } catch (Exception e) {
        logger.fatal(e);
        conn.rollback();
        throw e;
    } finally {
        conn.close();
    }
}
```

Notice in the above code that the connection logic that used to be in the DAO objects is now in the calling method. The connection is passed into the DAO, then used to get the statement and execute the update, and then returned back to the caller.

While this technique will work in most cases, connection passing is not an effective transaction design strategy. Using connection passing is error prone and requires a lot of program-

THE LOCAL TRANSACTION MODEL

ming effort to code and maintain. If you end up requiring code similar to the code above, then it is time to abandon the Local Transaction Model and use either the Programmatic or Declarative Transaction Model.

Local Transaction Considerations and Limitations

The Local Transaction Model works well for simple updates and small applications. However, once we add some complexity to our application this model breaks down. There are several limitations with this model that can pose serious restrictions on your application architecture.

The first problem with the Local Transaction Model is that there is plenty of room for developer error when coding the connection logic. The developer must pay very close attention to the auto commit flag settings, particularly when making several updates within the same method. Also, the developer must always be aware of the methods that are being called and if those methods are managing connections. Unless you have a simple application with mostly single-table updates, there is no effective way of making sure you are guaranteed of a single transactional unit of work for a single request.

Another problem with the Local Transaction Model is that local transactions cannot exist concurrently when coordinating multiple resources using an XA global transaction (we will see this in more detail in Chapter 5). When coordinating multiple resources such as a database and JMS destination (i.e. queue or topic) you cannot use the Local Transaction Model and still maintain ACID properties. Given these constraints and limitations, the Local Transaction Model should be used only for simple web-based Java applications that have simple table updates.

3

The Programmatic Transaction
Model

One of the biggest differences between the Programmatic
Transaction Model and the Local Transaction Model is that
with the Programmatic Transaction Model the developer
manages *transactions*, not *connections*. When using EJBs the
Programmatic Model is sometimes referred to as Bean-Managed
Transactions, or BMT. The term "BMT" is not used very often
because the Programmatic Transaction Model is applicable in
the Servlet Container as well as the EJB container and can be
applied to POJOs (not just EJBs). The following code illustrates
the use of the Programmatic Transaction Model using the EJB
framework with JTA (transaction logic is in bold):

```
public void updateTradeOrder(TradeOrderData order)
   throws Exception {
   UserTransaction txn = sessionCtx.getUserTransaction();
   txn.begin();
   try {
     TradeOrderDAO dao = new TradeOrderDAO();
     dao.updateTradeOrder(order);
     txn.commit();
   } catch (Exception e) {
     log.fatal(e);
     txn.rollback();
     throw e;
   }
}
```

In the above coding example the transaction context is propagated to the TradeOrderDAO object, so unlike in the Local
Transaction Model the TradeOrderDAO object does not need to

manage the connections or transactions. All it needs to do is get a connection from the connection pool and return it.

In the Programmatic Transaction Model the developer is responsible for starting and terminating the transaction. In EJB this is done through the `UserTransaction` interface. The `begin()` method is used to start the transaction, and the `commit()` or `rollback()` methods are used to terminate the transaction. In Spring this is done through the use of the `TransactionTemplate` or through the `PlatformTransactionManager` located in the `org.springframework.transaction` package.

Although using the Programmatic Transaction Model is generally discouraged, there are circumstances where it can be very useful. These circumstances are discussed in section 3.4. If we are using programmatic transaction in EJB, we tell the Application Server (specifically the EJB Container) that we want to manage transactions ourselves and use the Programmatic Transaction Model by setting the `<transaction-type>` node value to `Bean` in the `ejb-jar.xml` deployment descriptor. Normally the default for the `<transaction-type>` node is `Container`, indicating that we want to use Declarative Transactions (discussed in the next chapter). The choice of using the Programmatic or Declarative Model is done on a bean-by-bean basis. This means that you can mix the Programmatic and Declarative models. However, this is not a good practice and should be avoided.

For EJB 3.0 you can use metadata annotations and specify Programmatic Transaction Management by using the `@TransactionManagement` annotation as shown in the following listing:

```
@Stateless
@TransactionManagement(TransactionManagementType.BEAN)
public class TradingServiceBean implements TradingService
{
    ...
}
```

With the Spring Framework you have the choice of using the
TransactionTemplate or the PlatformTransactionManager. The
following code example illustrates the use of the more common
TransactionTemplate technique:

```
public void updateTradeOrder(TradeOrderData order)
    throws Exception {
    transactionTemplate.execute(new TransactionCallback()
    {
      public Object doInTransaction(
                      TransactionStatus status)
      {
          try {
            TradeOrderDAO dao = new TradeOrderDAO();
            dao.updateTradeOrder(order);
          } catch (Exception e) {
            status.setRollbackOnly();
            throw e;
          }
      }
    } );
}


<bean id="transactionTemplate"
      class="org.springframework.transaction.support.
              TransactionTemplate">
   <property name="transactionManager">
      <ref local="transactionManager"/>
   </property>
</bean>


<bean id="tradingService"
      class="com.trading.server.TradingService">
   <property name="transactionTemplate">
      <ref local="transactionTemplate"/>
   </property>
</bean>
```

As you can see from the above example, Spring uses a transaction callback that wraps the logic contained in the business
method into a transaction context. Notice that when using this
technique you do not have to explicitly invoke the begin() and
commit() methods as with EJB. Also, the rollback is handled
through the TransactionStatus.setRollbackOnly() method
rather than the Transaction.rollback() method used in EJB.

Obtaining a Reference to the
JTA UserTransaction

When using the EJB-based Programmatic Transaction Model in the client (either web-based or application), you must get the `InitialContext` and do a JNDI lookup when using EJB as shown below:

```
...
InitialContext ctx = new InitialContext()
UserTransaction txn = (UserTransaction)
    ctx.lookup("javax.transaction.UserTransaction")
...
```

Here is where things get a little complicated. The lookup name in the above code snippet (`"javax.transaction.UserTransaction"`) is *application-server specific*. This means that code in the client will most likely not be portable across application servers. Each application server binds the `UserTransaction` to a particular JNDI name. The following table lists the JNDI names for the most popular application servers:

JBoss	"UserTransaction"
WebLogic	"javax.transaction.UserTransaction"
WebSphere v5+	"java:comp/UserTransaction"
WebSphere v4	"jta/usertransaction"
SunONE	"java:comp/UserTransaction"
JRun4	"java:comp/UserTransaction"
Resin	"java:comp/UserTransaction"
Orion	"java:comp/UserTransaction"
JOnAS	"java:comp/UserTransaction"

To complicate matters, let's assume we are trying to access an EJB that is using declarative transactions from either an application sitting outside the container (non-web based) or from a JUnit test case. We could not use the following code example because in most cases the JNDI bindings are usually not available to code outside of the container environment:

```
UserTransaction txn = (UserTransaction)
   ctx.lookup("javax.transaction.UserTransaction")
```

This creates some problems when trying to test EJBs from JUnit or when accessing a transaction from a Swing-based application. The solution to this problem is to start the transaction using the `TransactionManager` interface. You would first load the application-server specific `TransactionManagerFactory` class using the `Class.forName()` method. Then, using reflection execute the `getTransactionManager()` method. This provides a transaction manager that can be used to start and stop the transaction. The following code snippet illustrates this technique using the IBM WebSphere `TransactionManagerFactory`:

```
...
//load the transaction manager factory class
Class txnClass = Class.forName(
   "com.ibm.ejs.jts.jta.TransactionManagerFactory");

//using reflection invoke the getTransactionManager()
//method to get a reference to the transaction manager
TransactionManager txnMgr = (TransactionManager)
   txnClass.getMethod("getTransactionManager",null)
                  .invoke(null, null);

//start the transaction via the transaction manager
txnMgr.begin();
...
```

Although the above example uses IBM WebSphere's `TransactionManagerFactory`, you could use this code for any application server by replacing the class name string in the `Class.forName()` method above with the one specific to your application server. This code segment can be added to a JUnit test case, application test client, or even in a Swing-based application requiring transaction control outside of the container environment.

For EJBs you can use the `SessionContext.getUserTransaction()` method for Session Beans or the `MessageDrivenContext.getUserTransaction()` method for MDBs. No casting is needed when using this technique. The code below shows an example of using the `SessionContext` to obtain the `UserTransaction` interface.

```
...
UserTransaction txn = sessionCtx.getUserTransaction();
...
```

Programmatic Transaction Coding Traps

When dealing with programmatic transactions developers must pay special attention to exception handling. Consider the code example below where we are ignoring runtime exceptions and only catching application (checked) exceptions:

```
public void updateTradeOrder(TradeOrderData order)
   throws Exception {
   UserTransaction txn = sessionCtx.getUserTransaction();
   txn.begin();
   try {
      TradeOrderDAO dao = new TradeOrderDAO();
      dao.updateTradeOrder(order);
      txn.commit();
   } catch (ApplicationException e) {
      log.fatal(e);
      txn.rollback();
      throw e;
   }
}
```

If we were to get a runtime exception (i.e. `NullPointerException`, `ClassCastException`) the container would handle this for us automatically and rollback the transaction. However, what would happen if we failed to handle any application or runtime exceptions in our code as shown in the listing below?

```
public void updateTradeOrder(TradeOrderData order)
```

```
throws Exception {
  UserTransaction txn = sessionCtx.getUserTransaction();
  txn.begin();
  TradeOrderDAO dao = new TradeOrderDAO();
  dao.updateTradeOrder(order);
  txn.commit();
}
```

In this example we are delegating all exception handling to the caller by the `throws Exception` in the method signature. If we were to get an application exception in the code above the following exception would be returned:

java.lang.Exception: [EJB:011063] Stateless session beans with bean-managed transactions must commit or rollback their transactions before completing a business method.

Using Programmatic Transactions means that developers are responsible for managing the transaction. A method that starts a transaction must also terminate that transaction. Since this is a runtime exception this error may not always be caught in testing, particularly with complex systems.

Now suppose we forget to code the `commit()` method in our Programmatic Transaction code as shown in the listing below:

```
public void updateTradeOrder(TradeOrderData order)
    throws Exception {
    UserTransaction txn = sessionCtx.getUserTransaction();
    txn.begin();
    try {
      TradeOrderDAO dao = new TradeOrderDAO();
      dao.updateTradeOrder(order);
    } catch (ApplicationException e) {
      log.fatal(e);
      txn.rollback();
      throw e;
    }
}
```

If we were to execute this code we would once again get the following error message:

java.lang.Exception: [EJB:011063] Stateless session beans with bean-managed transactions must commit or rollback their transactions before completing a business method.

As you can see from the preceding examples, when using programmatic transactions developers must pay close attention to transaction management as it relates to exception handling. The developer must ensure that the transaction is always terminated in the method that started the transaction. This is often times more difficult than it sounds, particularly for large, complex applications with complex exception handling.

The Transaction Context Problem

Within EJB (in particular Stateless SessionBeans) there is a serious architectural limitation in the Programmatic Transaction Model that I call the *Transaction Context Problem*. The transaction context problem is based on the restriction that you cannot pass a transaction context from one bean using programmatic transactions into another bean using programmatic transactions. However, you can pass a transaction context that originates from an EJB or client object using programmatic transactions into an EJB using declarative transactions.

Consider the scenario where we have two Stateless Session-Beans, EmployeeService and DeptService. The EmployeeService bean handles all functionality related to an employee (such as hiring an employee or giving an employee a raise). The DeptService bean handles all functionality relating to departments (adding, removing, and assigning employees). Both of these EJBs use programmatic transactions. Furthermore, assume both of these EJBs have corresponding DAOs. The following figure illustrates this scenario:

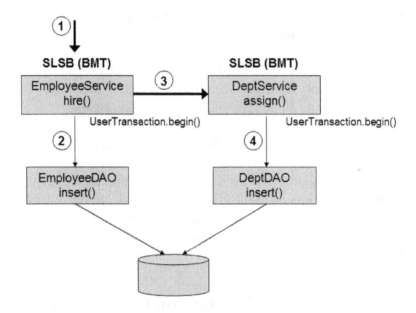

The *transaction context problem* occurs when using inter-service communication between services implemented as Stateless SessionBeans using programmatic transactions. Consider the example illustrated above. When we hire an employee we also assign that employee to a department at the same time. Therefore, the EmployeeService.hire() method invokes the DeptService.assign() method within the same business transaction. What we *expect* to happen is the transaction started in the hire() method should be propagated to the assign() method so that both operations are under a single transaction. However, this is not possible because we cannot propagate the transaction to the assign() method. Furthermore, the assign() method, which runs in a separate thread, starts its own transaction using the UserTransaction.begin() method because it can be invoked as an independent service. The following diagram illustrates this problem:

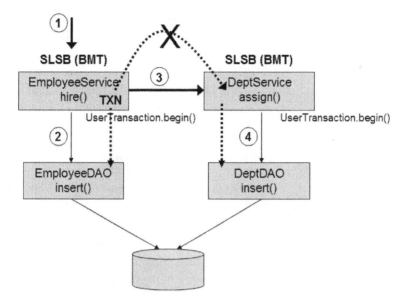

One major issue is that the *transaction context problem* does not show up in normal testing unless you specifically test for this scenario. What actually happens in the above scenario is the following:

- The `hire()` method starts a transaction and performs the necessary inserts and updates to the employee table via the `EmployeeDAO`.

- Next, the `hire()` method does a lookup on the `DeptService` and invokes the `assign()` method.

- The `assign()` method, belonging to a different SLSB, is started in a separate thread and starts its own transaction. The transaction started by the `hire()` method sits in a wait state until the `assign()` method completes.

- Once the `assign()` method completes the transaction started by the `assign()` method is committed (and thus terminated).

- Control is transferred to the `hire()` method and the original thread and corresponding transaction resumes.

In this scenario we do not have the atomicity or isolation properties of ACID, and hence no transaction management. If the original transaction started by the `hire()` method was rolled back after the `assign()` method was invoked the database would be left in an inconsistent state because the transaction started by the `assign()` method was already committed.

Programmatic Transaction Scenarios

Although the use of programmatic transactions is generally not recommended, there are many scenarios where the Programmatic Transaction Model is very useful. The most common use of programmatic transactions is *client-initiated transactions*. If a client is making multiple remote calls for a single business request, then the transaction *must* start at the client. When using JTA this requires the use of the `UserTransaction` interface and programmatic transactions. For client-initiated transactions you must use programmatic transactions on the client beans and declarative transactions on the remote EJBs. This is because the transaction context cannot be passed into a programmatic transaction managed EJB.

Another possible scenario is the use of localized JTA transactions. JTA transaction processing is very expensive in terms of performance and resource utilization. There may be times when you need to squeeze every ounce of performance out of your application (such as credit card processing). When valuable resources (such as a database or queue) are tied up, overall performance and throughput are affected throughout the entire application, not just a single thread. Therefore, to optimize performance you may choose to execute a majority of the code without a JTA transaction, and use JTA transactions only when necessary. Using the credit card processing example, you may not use transactions to do data loading, validation, verification, and posting. However, at the point when you transfer money from the account holder to the holding bank you would then start a transaction. That transaction would then be terminated once the account processing is finished, and the rest of the credit card processing completed without a transaction context. This is an example of *localized JTA transactions*. This is very difficult to do with declarative transactions due to the lack of programmatic control of when the transaction is started and terminated.

Another scenario is the use of long-running JTA transactions. In EJB long-running transactions are implemented through Stateful SessionBeans. There may be times when you want a transaction to span multiple requests to the server. In this case you would start a transaction in one Stateful SessionBean method and terminate the transaction in a different Stateful SessionBean method. While this is possible, it is a poor design because database or JMS resources are tied up for an extended period of time. Like localized JTA transactions this is not possible with the Declarative Model.

The Programmatic Transaction Model should only be used if you have a very good reason to use it. Three good reasons are for client-initiated transactions, localized JTA transactions, and long-running transactions. Aside from these scenarios you should use the Declarative Transaction Model.

4

The Declarative Transaction Model

As we saw in the Programmatic Transaction Model, the developer must explicitly start A transaction and commit or rollback the transaction using the `begin()`, `commit()`, and `rollback()` methods. With the Declarative Transaction Model the container manages the transaction, meaning that the developer does not have to write Java code to start or commit a transaction. However, the developer must tell the container *how* to manage the transaction. This is done through XML configuration settings in the `ejb-jar.xml` deployment descriptor and the extended deployment descriptors specific to each application server (EJB) or in the `ApplicationContext.xml` bean config file (Spring). In EJB the Declarative Transaction Model is sometimes referred to as Container-Managed Transactions (CMT), but most people prefer to use the *declarative transactions* term to keep the transaction model reference framework-agnostic.

From a Java coding perspective the only thing we have to worry about in EJB is coding the `setRollbackOnly()` method. This method tells the container that the only possible outcome of the current transaction is to rollback all updates, regardless of any subsequent processing. The following listing shows an example in EJB of the use of the `setRollbackOnly()` method. Notice that the lines in bold are the only Java code that involves transaction management:

```
@TransactionAttribute(TransactionAttributeType.REQUIRED)
public void updateTradeOrder(TradeOrderData order)
    throws Exception {
    try {
       TradeOrderDAO dao = new TradeOrderDAO();
       dao.updateTradeOrder(order);
    } catch (Exception e) {
       sessionCtx.setRollbackOnly();
       throw e;
    }
}
```

With Spring you do not have to explicitly code the setRollback-
Only() method. Instead, you can specify the rollback rules of
when to rollback the transaction in the TransactionAttribute-
Source interceptor. We will see examples of this later in this
section.

When using EJB, we tell the container that we want to use declarative transactions by specifying a value of Container in the
<transaction-type> node in the ejb-jar.xml deployment de-
scriptor. This is the default for most application servers.

In EJB 3.0 you can use metadata annotations to specify Declarative Transaction Management using the @TransactionManagement
annotation as shown below:

```
@Stateless
@TransactionManagement(
     TransactionManagementType.CONTAINER)
public class TradingServiceBean implements TradingService
{
    . . .
}
```

In Spring we would specify we are using declarative transactions
by using the TransactionProxyFactoryBean proxy. The following
example illustrates how to do this in Spring:

```
<bean id="tradingServiceTarget"
    class="com.trading.server.TradingServiceBean">
   ...
</bean>

<bean id="tradingService"
    class="org.springframework.transaction.interceptor.
        TransactionProxyFactoryBean">
  <property name="transactionManager" ref="txnMgr"/>
  <property name="target" ref="tradingServiceTarget"/>
  <property name="transactionAttributes">
    <props>
      <prop key="*">PROPAGATION_SUPPORTS</prop>
      <prop key="update*">
         PROPAGATION_REQUIRED,-Exception
      </prop>
    </props>
  </property>
</bean>
```

As you can see from the above example, using declarative transactions in Spring requires you to wrap the transactional bean with a proxy, as indicated by the code in bold above. Also, the use of the -Exception in the example above tells Spring to rollback the transaction on any Exception, eliminating the need to explicitly code the setRollbackOnly() method ourselves. Normally you would specify a specific checked exception type here, but for simplicity I am using the Exception class.

Transaction Attributes

When using declarative transactions we must tell the container how it should manage the transaction. For example, when should the container start a transaction? What methods require a transaction? Should the container start a transaction if one doesn't exist? The *transaction attribute,* located in the ejb-jar.xml deployment descriptor in EJB or TransactionAttributeSource bean in Spring, tells the container how it should manage the JTA transaction. There are six transaction attribute settings:

- Required

- Mandatory
- RequiresNew
- Supports
- NotSupported
- Never

Spring adds an additional PROPAGATION_NESTED attribute, which tells Spring to nest the transaction and use the Required attribute. Of course, to use this setting the underlying transaction service implementation must support nested transactions. Although the transaction attributes listed above can be specified at the bean level, transaction attributes are always associated with methods in a bean. When a transaction attribute is specified at the bean level all methods in that bean are assigned the transaction attribute value. This default attribute can be overridden using method-level assignment (we will see this later in the chapter).

REQUIRED

The Required attribute (PROPAGATION_REQUIRED in Spring) tells the container that a transaction is needed for the particular bean method. If there is an existing transaction context the container will use it; otherwise it will start a new transaction. This is the most common transaction attribute, and the one most developers will use for transaction processing. However, as we will see in the next section sometimes there are good reasons to use the Mandatory attribute instead.

MANDATORY

The Mandatory attribute (PROPAGATION_MANDATORY in Spring) tells the container that a transaction is needed for a particular bean method. However, unlike the Required attribute, this attribute will never start a new transaction. When using this transaction attribute, a prior transaction context *must* exist when the method is invoked. If a transaction has not been started prior to a method invocation, the container will throw a `TransactionRequiredException` exception indicating that a transaction is required but one was not found.

REQUIRESNEW

The `RequiresNew` attribute (`PROPAGATION_REQUIRES_NEW` in Spring) tells the container that it should *always* start a new transaction when the bean method is invoked. If a transaction has already been started prior to the method invocation that transaction is suspended and a new transaction is started. When the new transaction is terminated, the original transaction is resumed. Using the `RequiresNew` attribute violates the ACID properties of a transaction if there is already a transaction context established. This is because the original transaction is suspended until the new transaction completes.

This attribute is very useful for an activity that must be completed (i.e. committed) independent of the outcome of the surrounding transaction. One example of the use of this attribute is audit logging. For example, in most trading systems every action must be logged, whether that action succeeds or fails. Consider the situation in which a trader is attempting to place a trade for a particular stock. A JTA transaction is started for the `placement()` method. The `placement()` method invokes a common `audit()` method in another EJB that writes the attempted action to a database table. Since the `audit()` method is under the same transaction as the `placement()` method, the inserts to the audit table made by the `audit()` method would be rolled back if the `placement()` method is rolled back. This would violate the rule that everything must be logged in the audit table *regardless of the outcome of the action.* Therefore, assigning the `audit()` method a transaction attribute of `RequiresNew` would guarantee that the audit table updates were committed, regardless of the outcome of the surrounding `placement()` method.

SUPPORTS

The Supports attribute (PROPAGATION_SUPPORTS in Spring) tells the container that the method doesn't need a transaction, but if one is present it will use it. The Supports attribute is very powerful and very useful in transaction management. Consider a simple query to the database to get the total of all trades made by a particular trader. A transaction is not necessarily required to perform this action. Therefore, using Supports tells the container not to start a transaction upon method invocation. However, if this query is invoked during the course of an in-flight transaction, using Supports will cause the container to use the transaction context and look at the database log, thereby including any updates made during that transaction.

To illustrate the use of Supports, assume a particular trader is only allowed to trade up to 1 million shares a day. Using the Supports attribute the following sequence would occur:

Step 1: Total shares traded so far = 900,000
Step 2: Transaction Started
Step 3: Trader enters a trade for 200,000 shares
Step 4: Query with Supports invoked to get total shares traded (1,100,000)
Step 5: Exception thrown, trade limit for trader exceeded, transaction rolled back

Now, if we used NotSupported (described below), we would not get the exception because the query is outside the scope of the transaction and therefore does not see the attempted trade:

Step 1: Total shares traded so far = 900,000
Step 2: Transaction Started
Step 3: Trader enters a trade for 200,000 shares
Step 4: Query with NotSupported invoked to get total shares traded (900,000)
Step 5: Trade allowed, transaction committed.

NOTSUPPORTED

The NotSupported attribute (PROPAGATION_NOT_SUPPORTED in Spring) tells the container that the method being invoked does not use a transaction. If a transaction has already been started it will be suspended until the method completes. If no transaction exists the container will invoke the method without starting a transaction. This attribute is useful if there is processing that would possibly cause an exception if invoked with a transaction context. For example, invoking a stored procedure containing DDL code within the context of an XA transaction will cause an exception to occur. If changing the stored procedure is not an option, you could use the NotSupported transaction attribute as a work-around and suspend the transaction prior to the invocation of the method containing the problematic stored procedure.

NEVER

The Never attribute (PROPAGATION_NEVER in Spring) tells the container that the method being invoked *cannot* be invoked with a transaction. Notice the difference with respect to the NotSupported attribute. With the NotSupported attribute, if a transaction exists prior to the method invocation the container will suspend the current transaction and run without a transaction context. However, with the Never attribute, if a transaction context exists when the method is invoked the container will throw an exception indicating that a transaction is not allowed. Use of the Never attribute can lead to unexpected and undesired runtime exceptions, so this attribute should be used only when it is absolutely necessary. There are not many situations where this attribute would be useful. When in doubt, use the NotSupported attribute instead.

There are some restrictions regarding when these attributes can be used. As specified in the EJB spec, only the Required, Mandatory, and RequiresNew attributes can be used for Entity Beans. Message Driven Beans can only use the Required and NotSupported attributes. If an EJB implements the Synchronization interface, then only the Required, Mandatory, and RequiresNew attributes can be used. The Synchronization interface provides callback methods for the afterBegin(), beforeCompletion(), and afterCompletion() of a JTA transaction. This is useful if you need to perform functions during these events but do not have control over the transaction management. For example, Hibernate, an open source object-relational mapping (ORM) persistence framework (http://www.hibernate.org) uses the Synchronization interface during its transaction processing to integrate with JTA transaction management to invoke the Session.afterTransactionCompletion() method in the afterCompletion() callback to free up primary and secondary caching locks.

Specifying Transaction Attributes

Transaction attributes are always associated with a method, even if a default attribute is used for the entire bean. For EJB, transaction attribute values are specified in the ejb-jar.xml deployment descriptor as shown in the following XML example:

```
...
<assembly-descriptor>
  <container-transaction>
    <method>
      <ejb-name>TradingService</ejb-name>
      <method-name>*</method-name>
    </method>
    <trans-attribute>Mandatory</trans-attribute>
  </container-transaction>
  ...
```

Notice that all TradingService methods are assigned a transaction attribute of Mandatory (as indicated by the <method-name>*</method-name>). This is generally considered a poor practice because this technique is not optimized for query methods. For example, a getAllTradersByID() method does not need a transaction yet is always required to have one because of the default Mandatory setting.

In EJB 3.0, you can use metadata annotations and specify the transaction attribute as follows:

```
@Stateless
@TransactionAttribute(TransactionAttributeType.MANDATORY)
public class TradingServiceBean implements TradingService
{
     . . .
}
```

I will be using the EJB 3.0 annotation style throughout the rest of the EJB coding examples for simplicity. If you are using EJB 2.x, then simply replace the metadata annotations with the XML illustrated in the prior example.

In Spring, transaction attributes are specified by either using the `TransactionAttributeSource` or through the properties in a `TransactionProxyFactoryBean`. The following example illustrates both of these techniques:

Technique 1: Using the TransactionAttributeSource

```
<bean id="transactionAttributeSource"
      class="org.springframework.transaction.interceptor.
             NameMatchTransactionAttributeSource">
  <property name="properties">
    <props>
      <prop key="*">PROPAGATION_MANDATORY</prop>
    </props>
  </property>
</bean>

<bean id="tradingService"
      class="org.springframework.transaction.interceptor.
             TransactionProxyFactoryBean">
  <property name="transactionAttributeSource">
    <ref local="transactionAttributeSource">
  </property>
  . . .
</bean>
```

Technique 2: Using the TransactionProxyFactoryBean

```
<bean id="tradingService"
      class="org.springframework.transaction.interceptor.
             TransactionProxyFactoryBean">
  <property name="transactionManager" ref="txnMgr"/>
  <property name="target" ref="tradingServiceTarget"/>
  <property name="transactionAttributes">
    <props>
        <prop key="*">PROPAGATION_MANDATORY</prop>
    </props>
  </property>
</bean>
```

As you can see from the above example, the second technique is really a shortcut way of assigning the transaction attributes, and eliminates having to define the TransactionAttributeSource as a separate bean. When using the second technique Spring actually creates a NameMatchTransactionAttributeSource behind-the-scenes.

One technique related to transaction attributes is to specify them at the method level rather than at the class level. However, rather than explicitly assigning each method its own transaction attribute, a better technique is to assign a default transaction attribute at the class level and optimize other methods where needed. The best practice for doing this is as follows:

Best Practice:

When assigning transaction attributes to methods, make the class-level default transaction attribute the most restrictive attribute needed by the methods in the class, and then fine-tune methods as needed.

We can apply this best practice to the prior XML deployment descriptor example by making the default for all methods Mandatory and query methods Supports in EJB as indicated below:

```
...
<assembly-descriptor>
  <container-transaction>
    <method>
      <ejb-name>TradingService</ejb-name>
      <method-name>*</method-name>
    </method>
    <trans-attribute>Mandatory</trans-attribute>
  </container-transaction>
  <container-transaction>
    <method>
      <ejb-name>TradingService</ejb-name>
      <method-intf>Remote</method-intf>
      <method-name>getAllTradersByID</method-name>
    </method>
    <trans-attribute>Supports</trans-attribute>
  </container-transaction>
  ...
```

In Spring, we could apply this best practice as follows:

```
<bean id="tradingService" ...>
  ...
  <property name="transactionAttributes">
    <props>
      <prop key="*">PROPAGATION_MANDATORY</prop>
      <prop key="getAllTradersByID">
          PROPAGATION_SUPPORTS
      </prop>
    </props>
  </property>
</bean>
```

As we saw at the beginning of this chapter, EJB 3.0 simplifies
the setting of transaction attributes by using metadata annotations. Since the transaction attribute annotation can be applied at
both the class and method level, we could apply the best practice
above in EJB 3.0 as follows:

```
@Stateless
@TransactionAttribute(TransactionAttributeType.MANDATORY)
public class TradingServiceBean implements TradingService
{

@TransactionAttribute(TransactionAttributeType.SUPPORTS)
    public Collection getAllTradersByID() {
       ...
    }
}
```

Making the class-level default most restrictive is always safer because we are guaranteed of a transaction in the event a developer forgets to assign the transaction attribute to a new method. For example, if we reversed the examples above and made the default Supports and add a new update method without assigning a transaction attribute, it would not have a transaction context in the update method. This situation is often difficult to detect.

Exception Handling and setRollback()

Although the container or framework manages transactions when using the Declarative Transaction Model, in EJB there still is a small amount of Java coding we must do to make declarative transactions work properly. Consider the example below which places a fixed income trade, which is the purchase or sale of a security like a bond or treasury note:

```
@TransactionAttribute(TransactionAttributeType.REQUIRED)
public void placeFixedIncomeTrade(TradeData trade)
  throws Exception {
  try {
    ...
    Placement placement =
        placementService.placeTrade(trade);
    executionService.executeTrade(placement);
  } catch (TradeExecutionException e) {
    log.fatal(e);
    throw e;
  }
}
```

Here we have multiple updates within a single business unit of work. If we are in the middle of this method and a TradeExecutionException occurs, *the container will commit all work* done prior to the exception and propagate the exception to the caller. What this example illustrates is that *the container will not mark the transaction for rollback on an application exception.* Forgetting to handle application exceptions when using declarative transactions is a common source of data integrity problems in most applications.

To correct this problem we must tell the container to rollback the transaction on certain application (checked) exceptions. In EJB this is done using the setRollback() method in the EJBContext interface. In Spring this is done through declarative rollback rules in the properties of the TransactionAttributeSource bean definition. Using this method does not directly rollback the transaction; it only informs the container that the only possible outcome of the transaction is to rollback. Once this method is used the action of marking a transaction for rollback cannot be reversed. The code listing below shows the corrected code:

```
@TransactionAttribute(TransactionAttributeType.REQUIRED)
public void placeFixedIncomeTrade(TradeData trade)
    throws Exception {
    try {
        ...
        Placement placement =
            placementService.placeTrade(trade);
        executionService.executeTrade(placement);
    } catch (TradeExecutionException e) {
        log.fatal(e);
        sessionCtx.setRollbackOnly();
        throw e;
    }
}
```

With the setRollbackOnly() method added, the container will now properly rollback all prior database updates if the application exception occurs.

Although we must do some additional coding in our applications, it is important that the container does not automatically rollback the transaction on an application exception. For example, let's say that as part of some processing we need to send an email confirmation. If the SMTP server is not available, the SMTP service might throw an application (checked) exception. In most cases we would not want the container to rollback the entire transaction because we couldn't send an email. Catching the application exception and having control of the transaction allows us to make decisions about whether we can continue the transaction or roll it back.

When designing an overall transaction strategy for your enterprise Java application, one decision you must make is where and when to invoke the `setRollbackOnly()` method. The best practice for this is as follows:

> Best Practice:
>
> Transaction management should be contained within the method that starts the transaction. Therefore, only the business method that started the transaction should invoke the `setRollbackOnly()` method.

This practice is best applied when the transaction context is available to other beans or methods that are invoked from the method that started the transaction. This would occur in cases where inter-service communication occurs between transactional beans or the application contains multiple layers of transactional beans (i.e. session façade layer and persistence management layer). The rationale for this best practice is two-fold; first, based on a simple component responsibility model, transaction management should be contained in the method that started the transaction. Spreading transaction management throughout the application adds complexity and reduced maintainability of the application from a transaction management standpoint. Second, once the `setRollbackOnly()` method has been invoked, it cannot be reversed. This means that the method that started the transaction (and hence the method *managing* the transaction) cannot take any possible corrective action to resolve the problem and continue processing.

One corollary to this best practice is that methods not responsible for marking the transaction as rollback should provide enough information in the exception thrown so that the method that started the transaction can make the right decision about whether or not to invoke the `setRollbackOnly()` method. A good example of this is a checked exception indicating that a confirmation email could not be sent because the SMTP server is unavailable. In this case the method that started the transaction can post a pending email and commit the transaction. It would certainly be a shame to rollback every order just because the email server is down.

EJB 3.0 Considerations

The EJB 3.0 specification currently contains an `@ApplicationException` metadata annotation, which tells the container whether it should automatically mark the transaction for rollback when the exception is thrown. It takes as an argument a `boolean` value. The following listing shows the use of this annotation:

```
@ApplicationException(rollback=true)
public class MySeriousApplicationException
  extends Exception {
  ...
}
```

When a `MySeriousApplicationException` is thrown the container will automatically mark the transaction for rollback without the developer having to code the `setRollbackOnly()` method. The nice thing about this annotation is that we do not have to code the `setRollbackOnly()` method in our application. Also, unlike the `setRollbackOnly()` method, the container will not throw an IllegalStateException if there is no transaction context; it will simply ignore the request to rollback the transaction.

While this annotation tries to mimic Spring's rollback rule processing, using this annotation can have serious implications to your overall transaction design strategy. Because this annotation applies to a *class of exceptions* that any method could throw, any object, regardless of whether it started the transaction, will cause the transaction to be marked as rollback if it throws this exception. This goes against the best practice that only the method that started the transaction should be responsible for marking the transaction as rollback. If this annotation is used, no corrective action can be taken in the method responsible for managing the transaction. For example, if an SMTP email service method threw an exception containing this annotation, the entire transaction would be rolled back just because we couldn't send an email confirmation. Furthermore, use of this annotation with the rollback attribute mixes transaction management with exception handling, something that could cause additional problems further down the road.

setRollbackOnly() Alternative

In EJB, one alternative to using the `setRollbackOnly()` method is to throw a `javax.ejb.EJBException` system exception to force a rollback. This is a common technique that has its advantages and disadvantages. The following code illustrates the use of this technique:

```
@TransactionAttribute(TransactionAttributeType.REQUIRED)
public void placeFixedIncomeTrade(TradeData trade)
   throws Exception {
   try {
      ...
      Placement placement =
          placementService.placeTrade(trade);
      executionService.executeTrade(placement);
   } catch (TradeExecutionException e) {
      log.fatal(e);
      throw new EJBException(e.getMessage());
   }
}
```

Because the container will mark the transaction as rollback when a runtime exception occurs, this code will work the same as the code containing the `setRollbackOnly()` method.

The advantage of this technique is that it avoids a potential runtime exception when using the `setRollbackOnly()` method. If we use the `setRollbackOnly()` method and change the deployment descriptor associated with the code above to the `Supports` transaction attribute, the container would throw an `IllegalStateException`. The EJB 2.1 specification states the following:

"The container must throw the java.lang.IllegalStateException if the ejbContext.setRollbackOnly() method is invoked from a business method executing with the Supports, NotSupported, or Never transaction attributes".

Using the `EJBException` would avoid this runtime exception, but this is a poor reason to use it because it could hide a potential problem with our transaction design strategy.

One disadvantage of using the `EJBException` technique is the type of output produced by the `EJBException` verses the `setRollbackOnly()` method. The following output would be produced for an application exception involving a duplicate trade order using the `setRollbackOnly()` method:

```
WSCL0014I: Invoking the Application Client class
com.trading.client.ClientApp
Starting Trading Client
com.trading.common.TradingException: Duplicate Order
Duplicate Order
```

Using the same code, the output that is produced from the trading client when an `EJBException` is used is as follows:

```
WSCL0014I: Invoking the Application Client class
com.trading.client.ClientApp
Starting Trading Client
javax.transaction.TransactionRolledbackException:
CORBA TRANSACTION_ROLLEDBACK 0x0 Yes; nested exception
is: org.omg.CORBA.TRANSACTION_ROLLEDBACK:
```

Even though the same results are produced (i.e. the transaction is rolled back), the information about the duplicate order is lost by the time it gets to the caller.

Another disadvantage of using the `EJBException` technique is the lack of a proper separation of concern regarding exception handling and transaction management. A developer looking at the code may not realize that the purpose of the `EJBException` was to mark the transaction for rollback. Removing or modifying that logic might invalidate the transaction management strategy and may not rollback the transaction as originally intended. For these reasons I would recommend using the `setRollbackOnly()` method and avoid using the `EJBException` system exception as a means of transaction management.

Using Required vs. Mandatory Transaction Attributes

The decision to use the `Required` verses `Mandatory` transaction attribute is sometimes a confusing one. They both provide a transaction context, but the `Required` attribute will start a new transaction if one does not exist whereas the `Mandatory` attribute will not. Regardless of your transaction design strategy, the following best practice can help clarify when to use each attribute:

> Best Practice:
>
> If a method requires a transaction context but is not responsible for marking the transaction as rollback only, that method should have a transaction attribute of `Mandatory`

The rationale for this best practice is based on transaction ownership. With the exception of Stateful SessionBeans, the method that starts a transaction *must* be the same method that terminates the transaction. The management of a transaction, including when to mark the transaction for rollback, should always reside in the owning method. The use of the `Required` attribute creates a potential problem in that a transaction may be started by a method but not rolled back on an application exception. The most common scenario where this occurs is from client-initiated transactions. If the client starts a transaction and then invokes a remote Stateless SessionBean (SLSB), the remote SLSB should not be responsible for rolling back the transaction since the client was the one who started it. Therefore, since the SLSB component is not responsible for marking the transaction as rollback only, it should have a transaction attribute of `Manda-tory`. If the transaction attribute were set to `Required`, there is a *possibility* that a transaction may be started by the method but never rolled back.

The Reality of Transaction Isolation Levels

Another transaction setting available to developers is the transaction isolation level. *Transaction Isolation* refers to the degree in which interleaving transactions interact. It determines the visibility of updates a transaction will allow when other transactions are accessing and updating the same data. The DBMS (database), EJB, and Spring all allow you to set the level of transaction isolation. This setting, however, is both application server and database dependent. The application server may support various isolation level settings, but the database must also support those isolation levels in order for the setting to take effect.

Transaction isolation is a function of database concurrency and database consistency. As we increase the level of transaction isolation we in effect lower the database concurrency but increase the database consistency. The following diagram illustrates this relationship:

Isolation   Concurrency   Consistency

This setting can impact the performance and data integrity of an application. For example, for high-performance applications like credit card processing you can increase concurrency by lowering the isolation level (but impact data integrity). For low concurrency financial applications that have high data integrity requirements you can increase the isolation level, thereby increasing overall data consistency (but impacting performance). Most application servers and databases have default settings that balance concurrency and consistency. However, within EJB or Spring you can modify this setting to optimize you applications if needed.

Both EJB and Spring support four primary transaction isolation levels. These settings (from lowest isolation level to highest) are as follows:

- TransactionReadUncommitted
- TransactionReadCommitted
- TransactionRepeatableRead
- TransactionSerializable

TransactionReadUncommitted

This setting is the lowest level of isolation supported by both EJB and Spring. This isolation level allows transactions to read non-committed updates made by other transactions prior to those updates being committed to the database. To illustrate how this isolation setting works assume we have a particular stock currently trading at 90.00 per share. Two transactions (Transaction A and Transaction B) are trying to access the same data at the same time, with Transaction A performing updates and Transaction B performing reads. The following diagram illustrates how these transactions would interact using the `TransactionReadUncommitted` isolation level setting:

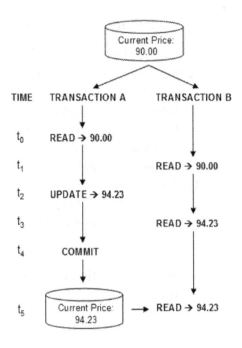

Notice in the diagram above that at time t_2 Transaction A makes an update to the database, but Transaction B is able to read that value at time t_3 prior to the update being committed to the database. As illustrated in this diagram, the updates for Transaction A are in no way isolated from Transaction B. If Transaction A were to rollback the updates, the data read by Transaction B would be incorrect. This isolation setting violates basic ACID properties and is not supported by many database vendors (including Oracle).

TransactionReadCommitted

This isolation setting allows multiple transactions to access to the same data, but hides non-committed updates from other transactions until they are committed. Using the same example above, assume the price of a particular stock currently trading at 90.00 per share. Two transactions (Transaction A and Transaction B) are trying to access the same data at the same time, with Transaction A performing updates and Transaction B performing reads. The following diagram illustrates how these transactions would interact using the `TransactionReadCommitted` isolation level setting:

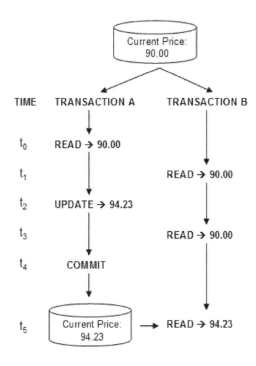

Notice that when Transaction A updates the data at time t_2 Transaction B does not have access to that data during the read at time t_3. This is a good level of isolation; it allows Transaction B to access the data (supports concurrency) but hides non-committed updates made by another transaction to the same data until it is committed. This is the default isolation setting for most databases and is supported by all database vendors.

TransactionRepeatableRead

Rather than interleaving the transactions, this isolation level setting keeps *all* transactions isolated from one another. This isolation level ensures that once a set of values is read from the database for a particular transaction, that same set of values will be read every time the select statement is executed (unless the transaction holding the read and write locks modifies the data). To illustrate this isolation level, assume we have a select statement that queries the database for all stock purchased so far today. Transaction A performs an insert during the course of Transaction B, which is performing the query. The following diagram illustrates how these transactions would interact using the `TransactionRepeatableRead` isolation level setting:

Notice in this example that although a new stock is purchased during Transaction B (stock QRS), the query performed by Transaction B returns the same results set, regardless of the update. Only when Transaction B commits will it see the stock that had recently been purchased. Note that with this isolation setting both read and write locks are placed on the data being queried and modified, so use this isolation level with care since transac-

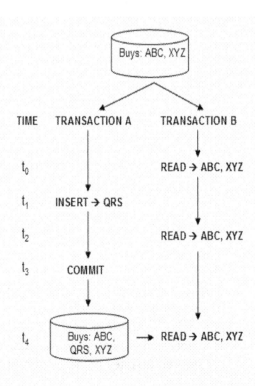

tions wanting to modify data read by a transaction using Repeatable Read will wait (or fail) until the transaction commits.

TransactionSerializable

This is the lowest level of isolation supported by Java. With this isolation setting interleaving transactions are "stacked up" so that only one transaction is allowed access to the data at a time (as we will see later in this section, this is not entirely true for Oracle). Concurrency is significantly impacted with this setting, but data consistency is significantly increased. Using the same example above, assume the price of a particular stock currently trading at 90.00 per share. Two transactions (Transaction A and Transaction B) are trying to access the same data at the same time, with Transaction A performing updates and Transaction B performing reads. The following diagram illustrates how these transactions would interact using the `TransactionSerializable` isolation level setting:

Notice that Transaction B is suspended until Transaction A completes. Although all database vendors support this setting, Oracle handles this setting a little differently. Since Oracle uses data versioning it will not actually suspend Transaction B. However, if Transaction B does try to access the same data during Transaction B, Oracle will return an `ORA-08177` error message indicating that it cannot serialize access for this transaction.

The Reality of Isolation Settings

In EJB the Isolation Level is an application server extension, and
therefore must be set in the application server-specific extended
xml deployment descriptor. Within Spring the isolation level is
set along with the transaction attribute. The following example
shows the settings for Weblogic (weblogic-ejb-jar.xml).

```
...
<transaction-isolation>
   <isolation-level>
        TransactionSerializable
   </isolation-level>
   <method>
      <ejb-name>TradingService</ejb-name>
      <method-inf>Remote</method-inf>
      <method-name>placeTrade</method-name>
   </method>
</transaction-isolation>
...
```

The following example shows the same settings using Spring:

```
<bean id="tradingService" ...>
   ...
  <property name="transactionAttributes">
    <props>
      <prop key="placeTrade">
        PROPAGATION_MANDATORY, ISOLATION_SERIALIZABLE
      </prop>
    </props>
  </property>
</bean>
```

EJB and Spring support for the transaction isolation is dependent
on the underlying database. Thus, although both frameworks
supports the four isolation settings discussed above, the database
must in turn support those isolation levels for the settings to take
effect. If the database does not support the setting specified in
the framework, the database default will be used. For example, if
you are using Oracle and use the TransactionRepeatableRead
setting in either EJB or Spring, Oracle will reject the setting and
use TransactionReadCommitted instead. Unfortunately no exceptions are thrown, so you may think you are using one setting

when in fact the database may override it and use another. Furthermore, when modifying the isolation level settings keep in mind your code may not be portable across database vendors due to varied support of the isolation settings.

It is best to avoid using anything but the `TransactionReadCommitted` setting unless you are sure the database will support the framework setting you want and you have a very good reason for changing it. The isolation level setting can play an important part of your transaction design strategy, but it should be used with care and caution.

5

XA Transaction Processing

To illustrate why the X/Open XA Interface is important in JTA transaction management and when it should be used, consider the following EJB coding example from the previous chapter where we placed a fixed income trade:

```
@TransactionAttribute(TransactionAttributeType.REQUIRED)
public void placeFixedIncomeTrade(TradeData trade)
  throws Exception {
  try {
    ...
    Placement placement =
        placementService.placeTrade(trade);
    executionService.executeTrade(placement);
  } catch (TradeExecutionException e) {
    log.fatal(e);
    sessionCtx.setRollbackOnly();
    throw e;
  }
}
```

This code first places a trade and then executes a trade, both of which update different tables in the database. As we saw in the previous chapter this code maintains ACID properties in a standard non-XA environment. Assume we were given a new request to send a JMS message to another system in the firm that had an interest in all fixed income trade activity. For simplicity also assume we placed all the details of the JMS logic in a method called sendPlacementMessage(). The code example above is modified as follows to add the new functionality:

```
@TransactionAttribute(TransactionAttributeType.REQUIRED)
public void placeFixedIncomeTrade(TradeData trade)
   throws Exception {
   try {
      ...
      Placement placement =
          placementService.placeTrade(trade);
      placementService.sendPlacementMessage(placement);
      executionService.executeTrade(placement);
   } catch (TradeExecutionException e) {
      log.fatal(e);
      sessionCtx.setRollbackOnly();
      throw e;
   }
}
```

While this change appears innocent enough, this code will not maintain ACID properties. If the `executeTrade()` method were to throw a `TradeExecutionException`, the database updates would be rolled back, but the placement message would be sent to the JMS queue or topic. As a matter of fact, the placement message would most likely be released from the JMS queue or topic immediately after the execution of the `sendPlacementMessage()` method.

Because the message queue inserts are independent of the database updates in a non-XA environment, the atomicity and isolation properties of ACID are not maintained and overall data integrity is compromised. What we need is a way to keep the message queue and database under the control of a single global transaction so that both resources are coordinated and act as a single unit of work. Using the X/Open XA Interface, we can coordinate the multiple resources and maintain ACID compliance.

The XA Interface Explained

The X/Open XA interface is a bi-directional system-level interface that forms the communication bridge between a *Transaction Manager* and one or more *Resource Managers*. The Transaction Manager controls the JTA transaction, manages the lifecycle of a transaction, and coordinates resources. In JTA the Transaction Manager is abstracted through the `javax.transaction.TransactionManager` interface and implemented through the underlying transaction service (i.e. JTS). The Resource Manager is responsible for controlling and managing the actual resource (e.g. database or JMS queue). The following diagram illustrates the relationship between the Transaction Manager, Resource Manager, and Client application within a typical JTA environment:

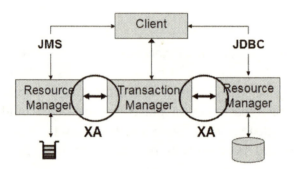

Notice from the above diagram that the XA Interface forms the communication bridge between the Transaction Manager and the various Resource Managers. Because of the bi-directional nature of the XA Interface, XA supports the two-phase commit protocol, which I will be discussing later in this chapter.

There is a lot more to the XA Interface than explained in this chapter. For those interested in taking a deeper dive into XA you can read the X/Open XA Interface specification in PDF format by going to http://www.opengroup.org/onlinepubs/009680699/toc.pdf.

When Should You Use XA?

A common confusion when using transaction management in Java is knowing when to use XA and when not to. Since most commercial application servers perform one-phase commit operations performance degradation is not a great concern. However, unnecessarily introducing XA database drivers into your application can produce undesirable results and errors, particularly when using the Local Transaction Model. Therefore, you generally want to avoid using XA when you don't need it. The following best practice describes when XA should be used:

Best Practice:

The X/Open XA Interface should only be used if you are co-ordinating multiple resources (i.e. databases and message queues or topics) *within the same transaction context.*

The important point here is that although your application may use multiple resources, you only need XA if these resources must be coordinated within the same transaction scope. Multiple resources would typically include accessing two or more databases (not tables, but separate databases), a database and a message queue, or multiple message queues. You may have an application that uses a database and a JMS message queue. However, if these resources are not used in the same transaction then you do not need XA. The coding example at the start of this chapter that placed a fixed income trade and sent a message to a queue is an example where XA is required to maintain ACID compliance.

The most common scenario where XA is used (and required) is the coordination of database updates and message queues (or topics) within the same transaction. Notice that these two actions can occur in completely different areas of the application (particularly when using an ORM like Hibernate). The XA transaction must coordinate both types of resources in the event of a rollback or to keep the updates in isolation from other transactions. Without XA, messages sent to a queue or topic are typically read by the receiver before the transaction even ends. With XA, the message in the queue would not be released until the transaction is committed. Another thing to note is that you do not need XA if you are coordinating an operational database with a database that is read-only (i.e. reference database). However, since XA supports the read-only optimization, you shouldn't see any overhead if you do need to include a read-only data source into your XA transaction.

There are many implications to consider when using XA in your enterprise Java applications. These implications include the two-phase commit process (2PC), heuristic exceptions, and the use of XA Drivers. The following sections describe each of these in detail.

Two-Phase Commit

The two-phase commit protocol (2PC) is the mechanism used by XA to coordinate multiple resources during a global transaction. The two-phase commit protocol complies with the OSI/DTP standard (Open Systems Interconnection), although it predates this standard by several years. The two-phase commit protocol consists of two phases; *Phase One* (the Prepare Phase) and *Phase Two* (the Commit Phase). A good analogy to describe the two-phase commit process is a typical wedding ceremony, where each participant (in this case the bride and groom) both must commit to the arrangement by stating "I Do" before they can be officially joined in matrimony. Consider the dire consequences if one of the "participants" decides at the last minute to back out of the commitment. The same consequences hold true with the two-phase commit process, although not quite as devastating.

When a `commit()` request is issued from the client to the transaction manager, the transaction manager starts the two-phase commit process. During Phase One all resources are polled and asked whether they are ready to commit their work. Each participant may respond with a READY, READ_ONLY, or NOT_READY response. If any of the participants respond with a NOT_READY in Phase One the entire transaction is rolled back. If all participants vote READY then the resources are committed in Phase Two. Participants that respond with a READ_ONLY are removed from the second phase of the protocol.

Two-phase commit is possible due to the bi-directional communication capabilities of XA. With non-XA transactions communication is only unidirectional and two-phase commit is not possible because the Transaction Manager cannot receive a response back from a resource manager. Most Transaction Managers multi-thread the polling process during Phase One and the commit process during Phase Two for performance optimizations and to free up resource as soon as possible. The following diagram illustrates the basic flow of the two-phase commit process:

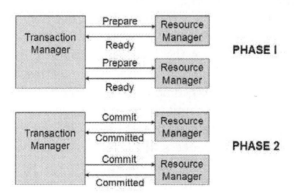

The diagram below illustrates the two-phase commit process when an error occurs in one of the Resource Managers (i.e. the DBMS) during the polling process in Phase One:

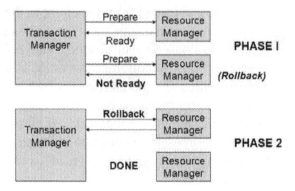

In this example a commit request was made to the transaction manager from a client running a *global transaction* (a JTA transaction running under XA). During Phase One the second Resource Manager responds back to the Transaction Manager with a NOT READY response. In this case the Transaction Manager issues rollback requests to all participants, thus coordinating all resources within the global transaction.

Some commercial containers offer a feature called the *Last Participant Support*, also known as the *Last Resource Commit Optimization*. Last Participant Support allows a resource that is not under XA to participate in the global transaction. With Last Participant Support, when a commit request is made to a Transaction Manager under XA the Transaction Manager will initiate Phase One with the XA resources first. Once the results from the XA participants are returned and tallied the Transaction Manager will then issue a commit (or rollback) request to the non-XA participant. The outcome of this request directs the rest of the two-phase commit process. If the request to the non-XA resource is successful the Transaction Manager will initiate Phase Two and make a commit request for the XA participants. If the request to the non-XA participant is unsuccessful, the Transaction Manager will initiate Phase Two and request that all XA participants rollback their work.

There are two problems with Last Participant Support. First, it is not portable across all containers. Second, because of the time lag between the end of the polling process in Phase One and the commit of the non-XA last participant resource, you may find an increase in *Heuristic Exceptions* (discussed in the next section) when using Last Participant Support. Because of these reasons, this feature should generally be avoided unless absolutely necessary.

Another optimization supported by most commercial application servers is the One-Phase Commit Optimization. If the transaction involves only one participant, Phase One is bypassed and the sole participant is instructed to commit. In this case the outcome of the entire XA transaction is based on the outcome of the sole participant.

Heuristic Exception Processing

During the two-phase commit process a Resource Manager may use *heuristic decision making* and either commit or rollback its work independent of the Transaction Manager. Heuristic decision making is a process that involves making intelligent choices based on various internal and external factors. When a Resource Manager does this it is reported back to the client through a *Heuristic Exception*.

Fortunately, heuristic exceptions are not that common. They only occur under XA during the two-phase commit process, specifically after a participant has responded in Phase One. The most common reason for heuristic exceptions is a timeout condition between Phase One and Phase Two. When communication is lost or delayed, the Resource Managers might make a decision to commit or rollback its work in order to free up resources. Not surprisingly, heuristic exceptions occur most often during times of high resource utilization. If you ever receive a heuristic exception in your application you should look for transaction timeout problems, resource locking issues, and overloaded resources as the source of the problem. Occasionally network latency or network problems may also cause a heuristic exception. Also, as explained in the previous section, use of the Last Participant Support feature will cause heuristic exceptions to occur more frequently.

The three JTA Heuristic Exceptions exposed through JTA are the `HeuristicRollbackException`, `HeuristicCommitException`, and the `HeuristicMixedException`. Each of these exceptions are explained through the following scenarios.

Scenario 1: HeuristicRollbackException during commit operation

In this scenario a client performs updates under XA and makes a request to the Transaction Manager to commit the current transaction. The Transaction Manager starts Phase One of the two-phase commit process and polls the Resource Managers. The Resource Managers report back to the Transaction Manager that they are ready to commit the transaction. However, between Phase One and Phase Two each Resource Manager independently makes a heuristic decision to rollback their work. Upon entering Phase Two a commit request is sent to each Resource Manager. Because the work has been rolled back between phases, the Transaction Manager reports a `HeuristicRollbackException` back to the caller.

When receiving this type of exception, the typical corrective action would be to pass the exception back to the client and have the client resubmit the request. We cannot simply re-invoke the commit request because the updates made to the database were removed from the database transaction log during the rollback operation. The following sequence of diagrams illustrates this scenario:

STEP 1: Phase 1 Processing (Prepare Phase)

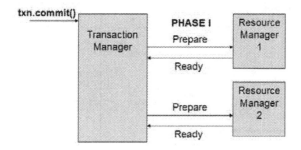

STEP 2: Between Phase 1 and Phase 2

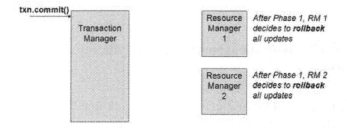

STEP 3: Phase 2 Processing (Commit Phase)

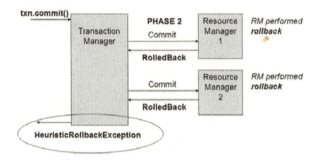

As you can see from the above diagram sequence both Resource Managers rolled back their work, even though they sent a READY response to the Transaction Manager during Phase One. Don't worry at this point why these exceptions occur; I will be going into this later in this section.

Scenario 2: HeuristicMixedException during commit operation

In this scenario a client performs updates under XA and makes a request to the Transaction Manager to commit the current transaction. The Transaction Manager starts Phase One of the two-phase commit process and polls the Resource Managers. The Resource Managers report back to the Transaction Manager that they are ready to commit the transaction. The difference between this scenario and the first one is that between Phase One and Phase Two some Resource Managers (i.e. the message queue) make a heuristic decision to *commit* their work whereas other Resource Managers (i.e. the database) make a heuristic decision *rollback* their work. In this case the Transaction Manager reports a HeuristicMixedException back to the caller.

It is more difficult to take corrective action in this scenario because we do not know which resources have been committed and which ones have been rolled back. The resources are therefore left in an inconsistent state. Since the Resource Managers operate independently from each other there is no coordination or communication between them with regards to their heuristic decisions. Handling this exception usually requires manual intervention. The following sequence of diagrams illustrates this scenario:

STEP 1: Phase 1 Processing (Prepare Phase)

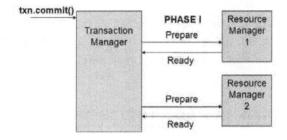

STEP 2: Between Phase 1 and Phase 2

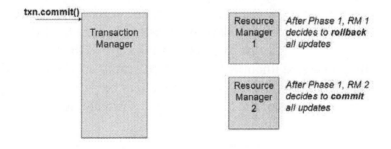

STEP 3: Phase 2 Processing (Commit Phase)

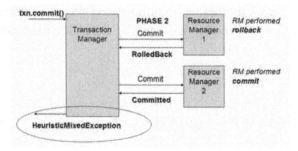

Notice in the above diagrams one Resource Manager committed its work while the other chose to rollback its work. In this case the Transaction Manager will report a `HeuristicMixedException`.

Enabling Queues and Topics for XA

Resources used under the XA Interface must implement the `javax.transaction.xa.XAResouce` interface to be included in the XA global transaction. For JMS destinations (queues and topics) this is done through the administrative console or configuration manager within the specific application server. What you are really XA-enabling is the JMS Connection Factory. When a JMS connection factory is XA-enabled a message sent to the JMS queue or topic will not be released until the end of the two-phase commit process. Without XA, a message sent to a JMS destination is immediately released and available to be picked up by the receiver, regardless of the outcome of the surrounding transaction.

JMS connection factories are XA-enabled in Weblogic by going into the administrative console under `Services` | `JMS` | `Connection Factories`. Under the Transactions tab there is an option labeled *XA Connection Factory Enabled*. Checking this box will XA-enable your JMS connection factory, thereby including the JMS destinations in a JTA global transaction. In IBM WebSphere, JMS connection factories are XA-enabled by going into the administrative console under `Resources | WebSphere JMS Providers | Connection Factories`. Checking the option labeled *Enable XA* will enable the JMS connection factory.

Enabling Databases for XA

Databases are XA-enabled through the use of XA database drivers. Since XA database drivers are more difficult to use than non-XA database drivers, they should only be used if you require XA in your overall transaction management.

Using an XA database driver can lead to unexpected errors that are often difficult to resolve. For example, switching from a non-XA database driver to an XA database driver can often produce errors that are very difficult to track. For this reason XA database drivers should be used during the development and testing cycle as early as possible.

The types of errors you might experience when using XA database drivers include local transaction errors and nested transaction errors. These errors occur when you try to start a new transaction while an XA global transaction is already in progress. This situation can occur in many circumstances, but the most common situations are mixing the Local and Declarative Transaction Models and using Stored Procedures under XA.

When using Stored Procedures under XA, errors usually occur when a DDL statement is encountered in the Stored Procedure (i.e. `CREATE TABLE`, `BEGIN TRAN`, `END TRAN`). This is usually the most common cause of XA errors and often the most difficult to correct. In Oracle, for example, you may see the following error occur when using XA:

ORA-02089: COMMIT is not allowed in a subordinate session

You will not encounter this error when using a non-XA database driver because the JTA transaction will be suspended when the

DDL statement is executed. Receiving this error is an indication that your Stored Procedure contains DDL code and that a local transaction (managed by the Resource Manager) is attempting to commit its work.

It is often difficult to remove the DDL statements from a Stored Procedure due to the nature of why it is being used or because the Stored Procedure may be shared by multiple applications. One effective workaround is to manually suspend the transaction prior to the invocation of the Stored Procedure, and then resume the transaction after returning from the Stored Procedure invocation. Using this technique will avoid XA-related local and nested transaction errors. However, the updates made by the Stored Procedure will be committed independently of the global JTA transaction, thus violating transaction ACID properties. This is why this technique is a work-around rather than a solution. The following code snippet illustrates this technique:

```
...
InitialContext ctx = new InitialContext();
TransactionManager tm =
(javax.transaction.TransactionManager)
   ctx.lookup("javax.transaction.TransactionManager");
Transaction currentTx = null;
try {
   currentTx = tm.suspend();
   invokeSPWithDDL();
} finally {
   if (currentTx != null)
       tm.resume();
}
```

Even though we are using declarative transactions we can use the TransactionManager to suspend and resume the transaction programmatically. This technique will avoid the SQL exceptions you may get when running under XA, but it really doesn't solve the core problem. The only real solutions are to remove the offending DDL statements from the Stored Procedure or use a JTA-based transaction service that supports nested transactions.

Summary

The most important concept in this chapter is to understand when you really need to use an XA database driver. Many architects and developers insist on using XA database drivers when in fact there is no real need to use one in the first place. If you are coordinating more than one updatable resource (database, queue, topic, or JCA) *within the same transaction* then you need to use the XA Interface. Otherwise, you do not need XA.

Another word of advice when using XA is don't always assume you have a faulty XA Database Driver when problems occur; chances are it is not the driver causing the errors, but rather your application code and transaction processing logic.

6

Transaction Design Patterns

The transaction models described in the previous chapters provide a framework for managing transactions in Java, but they do not address *how* to create an effective transaction management strategy. Developing a robust and effective transaction management strategy does not have to be a complex task. Using the transaction design patterns described in this book will simplify your transaction processing, allow you to build a more robust applications, and will give you a significant head start in developing an effective transaction design strategy for your application.

This short chapter is meant to provide a brief introduction to the transaction design patterns introduced in this book and describe what application architectures they typically apply to. This will allow you to identify which pattern is most applicable to your situation without having to read through all three patterns.

A Brief Introduction to the Patterns

A *Transaction Design Pattern* describes the overall transaction design strategy for a particular type of application architecture. Each transaction design pattern includes the type of transaction model that should be used, the transaction settings, the component type that should be responsible for managing the transaction, and finally the application architecture that is applicable for the particular transaction design pattern being described.

The transaction design patterns that are described in the next three chapters are the *Client Owner Transaction Design Pattern*, *Domain Service Owner Transaction Design Pattern*, and the *Server Delegate Owner Transaction Design Pattern*. As the names suggest, these transaction design patterns are based on a component responsibility model in which certain application component types own responsibility for starting and managing the transaction. These design patterns include many of the transaction management best practices described in the previous chapters. The purpose of these patterns is to apply a transaction template to your application to remove any doubt as to what component should be responsible for transaction management and what declarative transaction settings should be applied.

For most enterprise Java applications, you will typically use the *Domain Service Owner Transaction Design Pattern* to build a transaction management strategy. This transaction design pattern is the typical pattern that can be used for both EJB and Spring for transaction management. As you will see in chapter 8, this transaction design pattern relies on the declarative transaction model and is very simple to implement. It applies to enterprise Java application architectures that require remote access to backend service objects as well as simpler application architectures that do not leverage remote services.

When you are required to manage transactions in the presentation layer of your enterprise Java application, you should look to the *Client Owner Transaction Design Pattern* to design and implement your transaction design strategy. Although this pattern mostly apples to enterprise Java application architectures requiring remote access to backend services, it can also be applied to non-remote applications that contain local fine-grained service objects. This transaction design pattern is described in chapter 7.

The *Server Delegate Owner Transaction Design Pattern* is meant for enterprise Java applications that leverage the Command Pattern or Server Delegate Design Pattern. This transaction design pattern is a special case of the *Domain Service Owner Transaction Design Pattern* that solves many of the problems associated with client-based transaction management and EJB in general. It is the easiest pattern to implement, and can be applied to both EJB- and Spring-based applications. Chapter 9 covers this transaction design pattern and also briefly describes the Command Pattern and Server Delegate Design Pattern as it applies to this transaction design pattern.

7

Client Owner Transaction Design Pattern

A s the name suggests, in this transaction design pattern the *Client Delegate* component owns the JTA transaction. Although this pattern is primarily used when using EJB and remote Stateless SessionBeans with a web-based or Swing-based client, it can also be used for non-remote applications containing local fine-grained service objects when multiple requests to service objects are required to fulfill a single client request.

Context

Although undesirable, in certain situations it is necessary to force transaction management up to the client layer within an enterprise Java application. Consider the all-to-common situation where a single request is made from the client, but the client requires multiple (remote) calls to the server to fulfill that request. This situation occurs most often when domain services are too fine-grained and no aggregate services exist. When this type of situation occurs, we are required to push transaction management up to the presentation layer to maintain ACID properties.

Consider the following example where the client receives a request to placing a fixed income trade. An example of a fixed income trade is the purchase or sale of a bond or Treasury note, whereas an equity trade is the purchase or sale for a particular stock (like Google). When a fixed income trade is placed, the client invokes the `placeTrade()` method and the `executeTrade()`

77

method together within the same transaction. By contrast, these methods would be invoked independently for an equity trade. The following code snippet from a client business delegate object illustrates this scenario:

```
public void placeFixedIncomeTrade(TradeData trade)
   throws Exception {
   try {
     ...
     Placement placement =
         placementService.placeTrade(trade);
     executionService.executeTrade(placement);
   } catch (Exception e) {
     log.fatal(e);
     throw e;
   }
}
```

Because these actions must be treated as a single unit of work, they must be wrapped within a transaction. Without transaction processing at the client layer the code example above would not maintain transaction ACID properties because updates made by the `placeTrade()` method would be committed to the database prior to the invocation of the `executeTrade()` method.

While there are many ways to re-architect an application to avoid this trap, some situations still exist where an application must use client-based transaction management. One issue with client-based transaction management is that it usually places too much infrastructure-related responsibility on the client. This is particularly true if you are using a web-based framework that communicates directly with remote EJB Domain Service objects or remote Spring-based objects without using a business delegate object (refer to the Business Delegate Design Pattern for more information). One way to avoid having transaction management on the client is use either the Command Pattern or the Server Delegate Design Pattern. Both of these design patterns use the Server Delegate Owner Transaction Design Pattern, which is described in chapter 9.

Forces

- The client requires multiple remote or local calls to domain service objects to fulfill a single business request.

- ACID properties must be maintained, meaning that transaction processing is required to maintain data integrity.

- Domain service objects are fine-grained and no aggregate services exist to combine business requests.

- It is not possible to re-architect or refactor the application to provide a single domain service method invocation for a single client request for all client requests.

Solution

The solution for the client-based transaction management scenario is to use the Client Owner Transaction Design Pattern as the overall transaction design strategy. This pattern uses a component responsibility model that places the responsibility of transaction management on the client. The following diagram illustrates this pattern for both the EJB and Spring Frameworks:

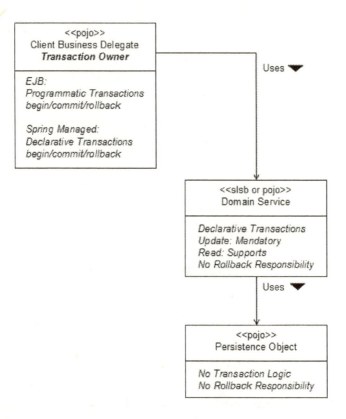

As the above diagram illustrates, the only component in the application responsible for transaction management is the Client Business Delegate (i.e. the *Transaction Owner*). If the Client Business Delegate is managed by the Spring Framework, then this component can use declarative transaction management. Otherwise, it must use programmatic transactions. For EJB this component must use programmatic transactions using the JTA `UserTransaction` interface described in chapter 3.

With this pattern the Domain Service component must use declarative transactions. As we saw in chapter 3, a transaction context established in the client cannot be passed into a remote or local domain service using programmatic transactions. However, a programmatic transaction context established in a client component can be passed to a local or remote domain service using declarative transactions.

Since the Spring framework provides support for transactional POJOs, a transactional context established in the Client Business delegate can be passed into a domain service managed by Spring, If using remote beans in Spring, you must use a remote protocol (i.e. RMI) that supports transaction propagation.

As the pattern specifies, all domain methods performing inserts, updates, and deletes must have a transaction attribute setting of `Mandatory`. Most importantly, the domain service objects *must not* mark the transaction for rollback for application (checked) exceptions. As described in chapter 4, marking the transaction as rollback is a form of transaction management that should be delegated to the component responsible for the transaction. In this case that component is the Client Business Delegate, *not* the Domain Service component. Marking the transaction for roll-back in the Domain Service components on application (checked) exceptions would prohibit the Client Business Delegate from taking any corrective action to possibly programmatically fix the problem and continue with the transaction.

Notice that this transaction design pattern calls for the use of both programmatic and declarative transactions in the same application. Although it is generally a bad practice to mix the programmatic and declarative transaction models in the same application, when using client-based transactions with remote services this is an acceptable and necessary practice (particularly when using EJB).

Consequences

- The client object managing the transaction must use programmatic transactions if using EJB, or can use declarative transactions if the client object is managed by Spring.

- If the server-based domain services objects are remote, the transaction must be able to be propagated to those remote service objects. For example, most of the remote protocols used by Spring do not support transaction propagation.

- Server-based domain objects must use declarative transactions since a programmatic transaction cannot be propagated to other programmatic transaction-managed beans.

- To maintain ACID properties server-based objects never start or commit a transaction. Also, server-based objects never mark a transaction for rollback.

- The transaction started by the client is propagated to any local POJO that is invoked within the scope of the transaction.

- Server-based domain objects must use a transaction attribute of Mandatory for all transacted methods.

- No transaction logic is necessary in the client or the server for query-related methods. However, server-based domain objects must have a transaction attribute setting of Supports for query methods.

- Persistence objects used by the Domain Service components, regardless of the persistence framework, must not contain any transaction or rollback logic.

- If EJB 2.1 Entity Beans are used, the transaction attribute for update operations must be set to Mandatory and no rollback logic used. For read operations the Entity Bean method should have a transaction attribute setting of Required for Container-managed Persistence (CMP) Entity Beans or Supports for Bean-managed Persistence (BMP) Entity Beans.

Implementation

The following source code illustrates the implementation of this pattern in both EJB and Spring. For purposes of the coding examples I will assume the Domain Service components for EJB are remote, and for Spring that both the Client Delegate and Domain Service components are managed under the Spring Framework.

Enterprise JavaBeans (EJB)

The source code for the Client Business Delegate component and EJB Domain Service component for **update operations** is as follows (transaction logic is in bold):

```
public class ClientModel
{
    public void updateTradeOrder(TradeData trade)
        throws Exception {
        InitialContext ctx = new InitialContext();
        UserTransaction txn = (UserTransaction)
            ctx.lookup("java:comp/UserTransaction");
        try {
            txn.begin();
            TradingService tradingService =
                ServiceLocator.getTradingService();
            tradingService.updateTradeOrder(trade);
            txn.commit();
        } catch (TradeUpdateException e) {
            txn.rollback();
            log.fatal(e);
            throw e;
        }
    }
}
```

```
@Stateless
@TransactionAttribute(TransactionAttributeType.MANDATORY)
public class TradingServiceImpl implements TradingService
{
    public void updateTradeOrder(TradeData trade)
        throws TradeUpdateException {
        validateUpdate();
        TradeOrderDAO dao = new TradeOrderDAO();
        dao.update(trade);
    }
}
```

Notice that the EJB Domain Service component does *not* invoke the setRollbackOnly() method on an application exception. Because we are not taking any corrective action on a checked exception, we do not have to code any try/catch block as we did in previous examples. As the best practice suggests in chapter 4, if the component does not start the transaction and is not responsible for managing the transaction, then the transaction attribute should be set to Mandatory and no setRollbackOnly() method should be invoked. Invoking the setRollbackOnly() method would be the only real reason to catch the checked exception in the Domain Service code.

As you can also see from the above code listings, the Client Business Delegate component uses the UserTransaction interface to start the transaction and performs the commit() or rollback() operations. With this pattern *all* transaction logic is contained in the client. Because the client is completely responsible for managing the transaction, the Domain Service component must never start a transaction, which is why it is assigned the transaction attribute of Mandatory. Because the declarative transaction model is used in the Domain Service component, a non-checked exception will mark the transaction for rollback. However, since the transaction context was started by the client, the container will only *mark* the transaction for rollback rather than actually rolling back the transaction. In this case, if the client tried to commit the transaction an exception would be thrown, indicating that the transaction has been marked for rollback and cannot be committed.

With this pattern there is no transaction context required on the client for read requests. Therefore, the Client Business Delegate component contains no transaction code for read requests. The Domain Service component is assigned a transaction attribute of Supports in the event a query method in the Domain Service component is used in the context of a transaction scope during an update operation (see Chapter 4). The source code for the Client Business Delegate component and EJB Domain Service component for **read operations** is as follows (transaction logic is in bold):

```
public class ClientModel
{
   public TradeData getTradeOrder(TradeKey key)
      throws Exception {
      TradingService tradingService =
         ServiceLocator.getTradingService();
      return tradingService.getTrade(key);
   }
}


@Stateless
@TransactionAttribute(TransactionAttributeType.MANDATORY)
public class TradingServiceImpl implements TradingService
{
   @TransactionAttribute(
      TransactionAttributeType.SUPPORTS)
   public TradeData getTrade(TradeKey key)
      throws Exception {
      TradeOrderDAO dao = new TradeOrderDAO();
      return dao.get(key);
   }
}
```

As shown in the above listings, from a transaction standpoint there is no code to write in either component. We only need to assign the EJB Domain Service method a transaction attribute of Supports. We also do not need all of the try/catch exception logic since we are not managing a transaction.

Spring Framework

The Spring XML configuration code for the Client Business Delegate component and remote Domain Service component for both the update and read operations using this pattern are as follows: (transaction logic is in bold):

```
<!-- Define the Client Delegate Bean -->
<bean id="clientModelTarget"
      class="com.trading.client.ClientModel">
  <property name="tradingService" ref="tradingService"/>
</bean>

<bean id="clientModel"
      class="org.springframework.transaction.interceptor.
            TransactionProxyFactoryBean">
  <property name="transactionManager" ref="txnMgr"/>
  <property name="target" ref="clientModelTarget"/>
  <property name="transactionAttributes">
    <props>
      <prop key="*">
        PROPAGATION_REQUIRED,-Exception
      </prop>
      <prop key="get*">PROPAGATION_SUPPORTS</prop>
    </props>
  </property>
</bean>

<!-- Define the Domain Service Bean -->
<bean id="tradingServiceTarget"
      class="com.trading.server.TradingServiceImpl">
</bean>

<bean id="tradingService"
      class="org.springframework.transaction.interceptor.
            TransactionProxyFactoryBean">
  <property name="transactionManager" ref="txnMgr"/>
  <property name="target" ref="tradingServiceTarget"/>
  <property name="transactionAttributes">
    <props>
      <prop key="*">PROPAGATION_MANDATORY</prop>
      <prop key="get*">PROPAGATION_SUPPORTS</prop>
    </props>
  </property>
</bean>
```

Because Spring can use declarative transactions for both the Client Delegate and the Domain Service components, the Java source code for both the update and query methods does not contain any transaction logic. The `setRollbackOnly()` is handled automatically by Spring via the `-Exception` in the above XML code. Notice that the rollback rules are missing from the bean specification in the `tradingService` bean. This is because we want to use the default behavior and not rollback the transaction on a checked exception.

```
public class ClientModel
{
    public void updateTradeOrder(TradeData trade)
        throws Exception {
        tradingService.updateTradeOrder(trade);
    }

    public TradeData getTradeOrder(TradeKey key)
        throws Exception {
        return tradingService.getTrade(key);
    }
}


public class TradingServiceImpl implements TradingService
{
    public void updateTradeOrder(TradeData trade)
        throws TradeUpdateException {
        validateUpdate();
        TradeOrderDAO dao = new TradeOrderDAO();
        dao.update(trade);
    }

    public TradeData getTrade(TradeKey key)
        throws Exception {
        TradeOrderDAO dao = new TradeOrderDAO();
        return dao.get(key);
    }
}
```

Notice the lack of transaction logic in both the client code and the server code. If the Client Model were not managed by Spring, it would have to have the same logic as with the preceding EJB example.

8

Domain Service Owner Transaction Design Pattern

The *Domain Service Owner Transaction Design Pattern* is the most commonly used transaction design pattern and applies to most Java-based application architectures you are likely to encounter. In this pattern the *Domain Service* component owns the transaction and all associated transaction management. In EJB the Domain Service component is typically implemented as a Stateless SessionBean and therefore uses the Declarative Transaction Model to manage transactions. In Spring the Domain Service component is implemented as a POJO and also uses declarative transaction management.

Context

Most architects and developers would agree that for enterprise Java applications the server layer should be responsible for managing transactions. The reasons for this are as follows: First, we may not know the type of client accessing the backend services. For example, a Web Services client cannot feasibly start and propagate a transaction to our domain service. Second, assigning responsibility for transaction management at the client layer typically places too much of a burden on the client, which should primarily be responsible for presentation logic, not server-based or middleware logic like transaction processing. Finally, performance usually suffers in client-based transaction management architectures because the client is typically making multiple remote calls to the server, which increases server chattiness and therefore degrades overall performance. Lastly, client-based transaction management adds unnecessary complexity to the overall transaction design strategy.

For these reasons, enterprise Java applications are usually designed with mid- to course-grained domain services that handle a single business request as a single unit of work. This simplifies the overall architecture and increases overall application performance. In this situation, the server-based objects take control of managing transactions. It therefore becomes a question of which components should be responsible for starting the transaction, committing the transaction, marking the transaction for rollback, and how the transaction should be propagated to the persistence framework.

Consider the example where a client is making a request to the server to place a fixed income trade. As we saw in the previous chapter, this request involves the invocation of a `placeTrade()` method and a `executeTrade()` method within the same transactional unit of work. Using course-grained services, the client code to perform this action would be as follows:

```
public void placeFixedIncomeTrade(TradeData trade)
    throws Exception {
    try {
        ...
        tradingService.placeFixedIncomeTrade(trade);
    } catch (Exception e) {
        log.fatal(e);
        throw e;
    }
}
```

Because the client is making a single request to the server, the client does not need to manage the transaction, even though we know this request will involve several server-based methods. Therefore, the transaction management must reside somewhere in the server-based objects.

Forces

- The client always makes a single request to domain service objects to fulfill a single client request.

- ACID properties must be maintained, meaning that transaction processing is required to maintain data integrity.

- Domain service objects are course-grained and/or use inter-service communication to perform aggregate service requests.

Solution

The solution for the typical server-based transaction management scenario is to use the Domain Service Owner Transaction Design Pattern as the overall transaction design strategy. This pattern uses a component responsibility model that places the entire responsibility of transaction management on the Domain Service components of the application, regardless whether the Domain Services are remote or local. The following diagram illustrates this pattern for both the EJB and Spring Frameworks:

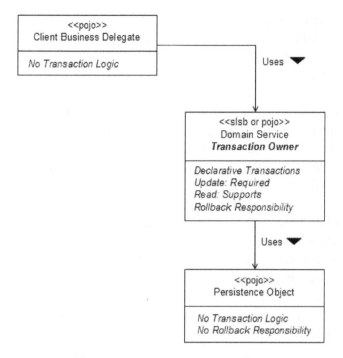

As the above diagram illustrates, the only component in the application responsible for transaction management is the Domain Service component. No other component type in the architecture is even aware that transaction processing is occurring. Regardless of the framework being used (EJB or Spring), the Domain Service components use the declarative transaction model and have a transaction attribute setting of Required for all insert, update, and delete methods, and a transaction attribute of Supports for all read operations. The core principle of this pattern is that the server-based entry point (i.e. the Domain Service method being invoked) owns the transaction, and therefore all objects referenced by the domain service are within the scope of the transaction.

The Required transaction attribute is used in this pattern for the Domain Service components rather than the RequiresNew transaction attribute in the event inter-service communication is used between Domain Service components (something that is fairly common in most enterprise Java applications). This transaction design pattern is fairly simple and relatively easy to implement and maintain because only the Domain Service component has transaction control logic, and therefore the coding and configuration effort is minimal.

Inter-service communication between Domain Service components poses an interesting dilemma with this pattern. Inter-service communication occurs when one Domain Service method invokes another method in a different Domain Service. Because the transaction attribute on all update-related methods is set to `Required`, if a transaction context is already established the method will use that transaction context rather than start a new transaction. However, if the inter-service method being invoked throws an exception, it may mark the transaction for rollback prior to leaving the method, thus not allowing the controlling method to take corrective action. While this is certainly a consideration to take into account, it does not significantly impact the transaction design pattern.

This is the most common transaction model used for enterprise Java applications. It should be used when the services provided by the Domain Service components are course-grained and the client only makes one request to the server for a single business request. Not only does this type of application architecture offer better performance than the multiple remote request architecture described in chapter 7, but transaction processing is placed on the server where it really should reside. This is particularly important when using web services clients or third-party client packages that are not easily modified.

Consequences

- The client (regardless of its type) does not contain any transaction logic and does not manage any aspect of the transaction processing.

- Since the Domain Service component is starting and managing the transaction, update methods must invoke the `setRollbackOnly()` method on application (checked) exceptions.

- Persistence objects used by the Domain Service, regardless of the persistence framework, do not contain any transaction or rollback logic.

- Server-based domain objects use declarative transactions and use a transaction attribute of `Required` for update-related methods and `Supports` for read operations.

- To maintain ACID properties client-based objects can never start a transaction, commit a transaction, or mark a transaction for rollback.

- Persistence objects used by the Domain Service components, regardless of the persistence framework, must not contain any transaction or rollback logic.

- If EJB 2.1 Entity Beans are used, the transaction attribute for update operations must be set to `Mandatory` and no rollback logic is used. For read operations the Entity Bean method should have a transaction attribute setting of `Required` for Container-managed Persistence (CMP) Entity Beans or `Supports` for Bean-managed Persistence (BMP) Entity Beans.

Implementation

The following source code illustrates the implementation of this pattern for both EJB and Spring. For purposes of the coding examples I will assume the Domain Service components for EJB are remote, and for Spring that both the Client Delegate and Domain Service components are managed under the Spring Framework.

Enterprise JavaBeans (EJB)

Unlike the Client Owner Transaction Design Pattern, this pattern has only one component type that contains transaction code (the Domain Service component). Therefore, since the client does not contain any transaction code, it is only necessary to show the Domain Service code for this pattern implementation. The source code for the EJB Domain Service component for update and read operations is as follows (transaction logic is in bold):

```
@Stateless
@TransactionAttribute(TransactionAttributeType.REQUIRED)
public class TradingServiceImpl implements TradingService
{
    public void updateTradeOrder(TradeData trade)
        throws TradeUpdateException {
        try {
            validateUpdate();
            TradeOrderDAO dao = new TradeOrderDAO();
            dao.update(trade);
        } catch (TradeUpdateException e) {
            sessionContext.setRollbackOnly();
            log.fatal(e);
            throw e;
        }
    }

    @TransactionAttribute(
        TransactionAttributeType.SUPPORTS)
    public TradeData getTrade(TradeKey key)
        throws Exception {
        TradeOrderDAO dao = new TradeOrderDAO();
        return dao.get(key);
    }
}
```

Notice that the `updateTradeOrder` method invokes the `setRoll-backOnly()` method on an application (checked) exception. Also notice that in keeping with the best practice described in chapter 4, the bean class has a default transaction attribute of `Required`, whereas the `getTrade()` read method overrides this default behavior and has a transaction attribute setting of `Supports`. Since no transaction context previously exists, the `Required` transaction attribute will cause a new transaction to be started on method invocation.

Spring Framework

With Spring this pattern is implemented exclusively through Spring's XML configuration file. The `setRollbackOnly()` method invocation found in the EJB implementation is handled through rollback rule directives in the bean config file in Spring. The configuration code for the Domain Service component for both the update and read operations using this pattern are as follows: (transaction logic is in bold):

```
<!-- Define the Domain Service Bean -->
<bean id="tradingServiceTarget"
      class="com.trading.server.TradingServiceImpl">
</bean>

<bean id="tradingService"
      class="org.springframework.transaction.interceptor.
            TransactionProxyFactoryBean">
  <property name="transactionManager" ref="txnMgr"/>
  <property name="target" ref="tradingServiceTarget"/>
  <property name="transactionAttributes">
    <props>
      <prop key="*">
        PROPAGATION_REQUIRED,-Exception
      </prop>
      <prop key="get*">PROPAGATION_SUPPORTS</prop>
    </props>
  </property>
</bean>
```

Because this pattern specifies the use of declarative transactions for the Domain Service components, the Java source code for both the update and query methods within the Domain Service component does not contain any transaction logic. As indicated earlier, the `setRollbackOnly()` logic is handled automatically by Spring via the `-Exception` rollback rule in the above XML code. The following code illustrates the fact that no transaction logic is required in the Java code for this pattern:

```
public class TradingServiceImpl implements TradingService
{
    public void updateTradeOrder(TradeData trade)
        throws TradeUpdateException {
        validateUpdate();
        TradeOrderDAO dao = new TradeOrderDAO();
        dao.update(trade);
    }

    public TradeData getTrade(TradeKey key)
        throws Exception {
        TradeOrderDAO dao = new TradeOrderDAO();
        return dao.get(key);
    }
}
```

9

Server Delegate Owner Transaction Design Pattern

This transaction design pattern is most applicable when using the Command Pattern or Server Delegate Design Pattern in your application architecture. With this pattern the Server Delegate component, which is the remote entry point into the server, owns the transaction and is responsible for all transaction management. No other component, including the client components, domain services components, or persistence objects, manages transactions or even knows that they are being used.

The Command Pattern is a useful design pattern that solves many issues with regards to client-based transaction management and EJB in general. The basic principle behind this pattern is that client functionality is placed in a *command* and sent to the server for execution. That command may contain one or more Domain Service method invocations. However, those Domain Service method invocations are all executed on the server via a corresponding *Command Implementation* object rather than on the client. Use of the Command Pattern allows you to make single requests to the Domain Services components from the client and also allows transaction processing to be managed by the server rather than the client.

The Server Delegate Design pattern is a similar concept, only rather than using a framework like the Command Pattern, this pattern simply places the client-side business delegate logic in Server-based delegate objects on the server. The end results are the same; transaction processing is moved to the server and multiple requests to the server for a single client request are reduced to one.

The Server Delegate Owner transaction design pattern is a special case of the Domain Service Owner Transaction Design Pattern. The main difference between the patterns is that when used with the Command Pattern this pattern has a *single object* that owns the transaction rather than a *component type* that owns the transaction. For example, if your application has 40 Domain Service Components, with the Domain Service Owner pattern you would have *40 beans* managing transactions, whereas you would only have *one bean* (the Command Processor) managing transactions with this pattern.

Context

Consider the following code example in EJB where a client object must make multiple calls to the server to fulfill as single business request:

```
public class ClientModel
{
   public void placeFixedIncomeTrade(TradeData trade)
      throws Exception {
      InitialContext ctx = new InitialContext();
      UserTransaction txn = (UserTransaction)
         ctx.lookup("java:comp/UserTransaction");
      try {
         txn.begin();
         ...
         Placement placement =
            placementService.placeTrade(trade);
         executionService.executeTrade(placement);
         txn.commit();
      } catch (TradeUpdateException e) {
         txn.rollback();
         log.fatal(e);
         throw e;
      }
   }
}
```

In this case the client must use programmatic transactions to ensure ACID properties are met within a single transactional unit of work. In this situation, not only is the client responsible for transaction management, but performance is impacted because of the multiple calls to (remote) domain services. Furthermore, in this example Domain Service objects are written in EJB as Stateless SessionBeans, further complicating the architecture.

In a move towards simplifying this type of situation, we would refactor the Stateless SessionBean Domain Services to POJOs, remove transaction logic from the client, and only make a single call to the server for any given client request. We could apply either the Command Pattern or Server Delegate Design Pattern to achieve any or all of these goals. When applying either of these patterns, transaction processing that originally resided in the client layer is now moved to the server layer. The following example shows the transformed client using the Command Pattern:

```
public class ClientModel
{
    public void placeFixedIncomeTrade(TradeData trade)
        throws Exception {
        PlaceFITradeCommand command =
            new PlaceFITradeCommand();
        command.setTrade(trade);
        CommandHandler.execute(command);
    }
}
```

This is a much more simplified version of the previous code. However, the question remains as to where to place the transaction processing logic. In this scenario the Server Delegate Owner Transaction Design Pattern can be used to identify the components that should be responsible for transaction management and what the declarative transaction settings should be for those components.

Forces

- The Command Pattern or Server Delegate Design Pattern is used in the application architecture for client/server communication.

- The client always makes a single request to a Server Delegate to fulfill a single client request.

- ACID properties must be maintained, meaning that transaction processing is required to maintain data integrity.

- Domain service objects are implemented as POJOs and may be remote or local.

- The Command Processor or Server Delegate is the only entry point into the domain services from the client.

Solution

When using the Command Pattern or Server Delegate Design Pattern, the Server Delegate Owner Transaction Design Pattern can be used to specify the overall transaction design strategy for this type of application architecture. This pattern uses a component responsibility model that places the entire responsibility of transaction management on the Server Delegate component. When using the Command Pattern the Server Delegate component is implemented as a single *Command Processor* component that locates the corresponding command implementation object and executes the command. In EJB this component would typically be implemented as a Stateless SessionBean. In Spring, it would be implemented as a Spring-managed bean (POJO). When using the Server Delegate Design pattern each functional group of client requests would be implemented as a separate Server Delegate (either a POJO in Spring or a SLSB in EJB).

The following diagram illustrates this pattern for both the EJB and Spring Frameworks:

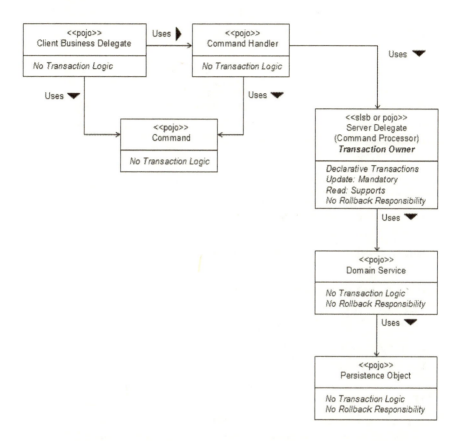

The Server Delegate component uses declarative transactions and is assigned a transaction attribute of `Required` for update methods and `Supports` for all read methods. The Server Delegate component also invokes the `setRollbackOnly()` in update methods for application exceptions.

The application architectures that are used with this pattern are very unique. In the case of the Command Pattern, the Server Delegate is usually implemented as a Command Processor and simply accepts a Command object from the client and executes that command. Use of interfaces throughout the Command Pattern framework ensures that the Command Handler component,

Command Processor component, Command Implementation Interface, and Command Interface all remain generic and application agnostic. The transaction context established by the Server Delegate is propagated to all objects that are invoked by the Server Delegate.

In the Server Delegate Design Pattern, the Server Delegate components act as a client façade to the Domain Services components of the application architecture. In this design pattern the client logic is essentially moved to the server and placed in the Server Delegate components.

The main drawback of these design patterns is that the Server Delegate component contains client-based logic rather than pure server-based logic. In addition, it is often difficult to implement this design pattern because the client business delegate is often times tightly bound with the web framework being used. A good example of this is in Struts, where the Action class can (and most of the times does) act as the client business delegate. Furthermore, it may be difficult to move client logic because code containing references to client-based objects such as `HTTPSession`, `HTTPRequest`, and `HTTPResponse` cannot be easily moved to the server.

However, one clear advantage of either of these design patterns is that the Domain Services components, which contain most of the business logic to process a request, are implemented as POJOs (Plain Old Java Objects) rather than EJBs. Domain Service components are therefore decoupled from the EJB framework, making them much easier to test. Another unique aspect about the Server Delegate Owner transaction design pattern is that since the server delegate is usually implemented as a singleton Stateless SessionBean component, the transaction logic for the entire application resides in a single object. As a result, this is the simplest transaction design pattern to implement and maintain. Furthermore, this transaction design pattern places the burden and responsibility of transaction management a level above the Domain Service components, freeing the core server functionality of the application from infrastructure-related aspects such as transaction management. With this transaction design pattern Domain Service components can be written as POJOs, and since they do not contain transaction logic they are easier to test outside of the container environment.

Consequences

- The client (regardless of its type) does not contain any transaction logic and does not manage any aspect of the transaction processing.

- Since the Server Delegate component is starting and managing the transaction, update methods must invoke the `setRollbackOnly()` method on application exceptions.

- The transaction established by the Server Delegate is propagated to the POJO-based Domain Services objects as well as the Persistence objects used by the Domain Service (regardless of the persistence framework). Furthermore, none of these components contain any transaction or rollback logic.

- Server Delegate objects use declarative transactions and use a transaction attribute of `Required` for update-related methods and `Supports` for read operations.

- To maintain ACID properties client-based objects can never start a transaction, commit a transaction, or mark a transaction for rollback.

- Persistence objects and Domain Services do not contain any transaction or rollback logic.

- If EJB 2.1 Entity Beans are used, the transaction attribute for update operations must be set to `Mandatory` and no rollback logic is used. For read operations the Entity Bean method should have a transaction attribute setting of `Required` for Container-managed Persistence (CMP)

Entity Beans or supports for Bean-managed Persistence (BMP) Entity Beans.

Implementation

The following source code illustrates the implementation of this pattern for both EJB and Spring. For purposes of the coding examples I will assume the Command Pattern is used. For EJB I will assume the Command Processor is implemented as Stateless SessionBean, and for Spring I will assume that the Command Processor is managed under the Spring Framework.

Enterprise JavaBeans (EJB)

Under the Command Pattern this transaction design pattern has only one component that contains transaction code (the Command Processor component). Therefore, since the client does not contain any transaction code, it is only necessary to show the Server Delegate (Command Processor) code for this pattern implementation. The source code for the EJB Domain Service component for update and read operations is as follows (transaction logic is in bold):

```
@Stateless
public class CommandProcessorImpl
    implements CommandProcessor
{
    @TransactionAttribute(
        TransactionAttributeType.SUPPORTS)
    public BaseCommand executeRead(BaseCommand command)
        throws Exception {
        CommandImpl implementationClass =
            getCommandImpl(command);
        return implementationClass.execute(command);
    }

    @TransactionAttribute(
        TransactionAttributeType.REQUIRED)
    public BaseCommand executeUpdate(BaseCommand command)
        throws Exception {
        try {
```

```
        CommandImpl implementationClass =
            getCommandImpl(command);
        return implementationClass.execute(command);
    } catch (Exception e) {
        sessionCtx.setRollbackOnly();
        throw e;
    }
  }
}
```

The getCommandImpl() method in the above example uses reflection to load and instantiate the command implementation object. It is then executed, and the results passed back to the client via the Command object. Notice that this implementation is very much like the Domain Service Owner transaction design pattern in that we use a transaction attribute of Supports for read operations and a transaction attribute of Required coupled with the setRollbackOnly() method for update-related methods.

SPRING FRAMEWORK

With Spring this pattern is implemented exclusively through Spring's XML configuration file. The `setRollbackOnly()` method invocation found in the EJB implementation is handled through rollback rule directives in the config file in Spring. The configuration code for the Server Delegate (Command Processor) component for both the update and read operations using this pattern are as follows: (transaction logic is in bold):

```
<!-- Define the Server Delegate Command Processor -->
<bean id="commandProcessorTarget"
      class="com.commandframework.server.
             commandProcessorImpl">
</bean>

<bean id="commandProcessor"
      class="org.springframework.transaction.interceptor.
             TransactionProxyFactoryBean">
  <property name="transactionManager" ref="txnMgr"/>
  <property name="target" ref="tradingServiceTarget"/>
  <property name="transactionAttributes">
    <props>
      <prop key="executeUpdate">
        PROPAGATION_REQUIRED,-Exception
      </prop>
      <prop key="executeRead">
        PROPAGATION_SUPPORTS
      </prop>
    </props>
  </property>
</bean>
```

Because this pattern specifies the use of declarative transactions for the Server Delegate component, the Java source code for both the update and query methods within the Domain Service component does not contain any transaction logic. As indicated earlier, the `setRollbackOnly()` logic is handled automatically by Spring via the `-Exception` in the above XML code. The following code illustrates the lack of transaction logic in the Spring implementation of this pattern:

```
public class CommandProcessorImpl
    implements CommandProcessor
{
   public BaseCommand executeRead(BaseCommand command)
      throws Exception {
      CommandImpl implementationClass =
         getCommandImpl(command);
      return implementationClass.execute(command);
   }

   public BaseCommand executeUpdate(BaseCommand command)
      throws Exception {
      CommandImpl implementationClass =
         getCommandImpl(command);
      return implementationClass.execute(command);
   }
}
```

Notice in the case of the Spring implementation both of these methods do the exact same thing, and unlike the EJB implementation, exception handling is not required because the setRollbackOnly logic in contained in the rollback rules in XML.

10

Summary

B y understanding each of the three transaction models and using the transaction design patterns described in this book, you can simplify your transaction processing and create a more effective and robust transaction design strategy for your application. Transaction processing is very important and also necessary to maintain data integrity in both your application and database. Transaction management in Java does not have to be complicated; using the transaction design patterns described in this chapter makes transaction processing easy to understand, implement, and maintain.

About the Author

Mark Richards is Certified Senior IT Architect at IBM, where he is involved in the architecture and design of large-scale Service Oriented Architectures in J2EE and other technologies, primarily in the financial services industry. He has been involved in the software industry as a developer, designer, and architect since 1984, and has significant experience and expertise in J2EE architecture and development, Object-oriented design and development, and systems integration. Mark served as the President of the Boston Java User Group in 1997 and 1998, and the President of the New England Java Users Group from 1999 thru 2003. Besides this book he is one of the contributing authors of the upcoming book "NFJS Anthology 2006 Edition" (June 2006), and also contributing author of the Java Coding Standards book produced by the New England Java Users Group Coding Standards SIG. Mark is an IBM Certified Application Architect, Sun Certified J2EE Business Component Developer, a Sun Certified J2EE Enterprise Architect, a Sun Certified Java Programmer, a BEA WebLogic Certified Developer, a Certified Java Instructor, and holds a Masters Degree in Computer Science from Boston University. Mark is a regular conference speaker at the No Fluff Just Stuff Symposium Series and frequently speaks at user groups and other conferences around the country.

www.ingramcontent.com/pod-product-compliance
Lightning Source LLC
Chambersburg PA
CBHW051253050326
40689CB00007B/1179